Mirror on the Veil

A Collection of Personal Essays on Hijab and Veiling

Edited by Nausheen Pasha-Zaidi and Shaheen Pasha

Critical, Cultural and Communications Press
London
2017

Mirror on the Veil: A Collection of Personal Essays on Hijab and Veiling
Edited by Nausheen Pasha-Zaidi and Shaheen Pasha

The rights of Nausheen Pasha-Zaidi and Shaheen Pasha to be identified as editors of this work have been asserted by them in accordance with the Copyright, Designs and Patents Act, 1988.

First published in Great Britain by Critical, Cultural and Communications Press, 2017.

Cover design by Hannibal.

ISBN 9781905510511

CONTENTS

Acknowledgments

We would like to thank first and foremost all the contributors to this anthology. Without your willingness to share your lives and your thoughts, this collection would still be a figment of our imagination. We would also like to thank all the reviewers who took the time to provide feedback for the essays, especially Karen Sargent and Alan Davis, who reviewed many of the submissions. Special thanks to Nadia Eldermerdash, who not only contributed, but also reviewed nearly all of the essays, even those that did not make it to the final collection. We are extremely grateful to Imam Tahir Anwar, Imam at the Islamic Center of San Jose, who helped provide some of the context behind the Islamic words and concepts defined in the glossary.

Mirror on the Veil
Ansha Zaman

I am from blue and black and magenta fabrics of cotton and satin and chiffon.

I am from a rusty green *almirah* that a certain Nani kept all her hidden treasures in and the labors of a *dorji* who never quite knew how to get the seams right.

I am from endless walks to Chandni Chowk on hot summer Dhaka days to find the perfect matching brooch.

I am from the smell of *itar* on Eid and from the stains of Rajshahi mango pulp dripping down the chin.

I am from the love of a paranoid mother who won't let her daughter leave the house without a salaam and a hurried prayer.

I am from the teachings of a father who cares only about what his daughter thinks and not what she wears.

I am from that young woman's love affair with Islam, with God.

I am from choice.

I am from the privilege that comes with having that choice when there are so many women who don't.

I am from the frustration that comes with justifying that choice to those who are not entitled to it.

I am from the refusal to become another broken/oppressed soul saved by the "good natured" colonialists next door.

I am from the rebellion against white imperialist ideals of beauty.

I am from ties with innocence, with childhood and a home always so far away and always so close.

I am from comfort, I am from habit in a land that is alien.

I am from faith, from resistance, from the heart.

Introduction
Nausheen Pasha-Zaidi

> *"Look directly into every mirror.*
> *Realize our reflection is the first sentence to a story, and our story starts:*
> *We were here."*
> ~ Shane Koyczan

I currently do not wear a headscarf, although I have in the past. This has caused quite a bit of consternation among many when discussing my research interests in hijab and veiling. While working on my Ph.D. dissertation, I was asked why I would want to pursue this line of enquiry considering that I am not a Muslim woman who covers, *per se*. And for the last few years, while working on this collection, I have felt that perhaps my lack of a headscarf has made it more difficult for some people to trust me with their words. Recently, a student asked me if I was interested in this topic because somehow I felt guilty for not wearing the headscarf as a sign of my religious affiliation.

Actually, I have been interested in head cover for almost thirty years, when at the age of sixteen, a medical condition forced me to watch my hair slowly float into the washbasin, leaving me with an unusually wide side parting and wispy strands that did not suitably cover my head. At the time, some of my Pakistani friends and acquaintances were finding a voice and an identity through the headscarf. For me, though, it was merely a visible representation of religion, which was (and continues to be to some extent) a private matter. So, instead of being a part of the new found freedom that my friends enjoyed in the hijab, I lamented the loss of my hair as the loss of my femininity and the loss of my potential career in broadcasting. I began to pray, many times reading and re-reading the prayers in the hopes of perfecting my communication with God. And I begged Him to give me back my hair. For many years, I struggled with this loss. I gave up on my dream of being on TV, although I did do some work on ethnic television for a while, which gave me a small taste of the world that I could not be a part of. Eventually, I realized that I wasn't cut out for a career in broadcast media with its unrealistic standards of beauty. I wasn't going to make it. I didn't have the right look – I didn't have the hair.

But the loss had brought me closer to my religion and I had learned to embrace the simplicity that I found in having a direct relationship with God. I fought to overcome my obsession with rituals and became more interested in the spirit of my faith. At one time, I felt that I needed to express my faith through the headscarf. At this point in the United States and in many other countries around the world, the hijab had become more or less equated with a Muslim woman. This was in the early 2000s. The headscarf was no longer seen as a reflection of the traditional immigrant woman or as a fad among young girls searching for an identity.

So, I tried it. And I loved looking Muslim – for a while.

But I am a person who needs constant change. Embracing change is the only thing that has been constant in my life. Although I removed the headscarf after only six months, my faith did not fade. In fact, it kept me afloat as an expatriate crossing national and international boundaries, creating new homes, saying goodbye to new friends, and hello to even newer ones. My faith was, and continues to be, a huge part of who I am. It is what keeps me breathing.

But as I no longer wear the headscarf, my faith has become almost a hidden entity to others, invisible under the strands of hair from the extensions that cover my head. So, you see, my interest in the headscarf is not a simple thing that can easily be explained to people in passing. I am grateful for this journey that has led me to consider the diverse aspects of who I am — a Muslim, a woman, a Pakistani and an American, a teacher, an academic, and a person of colour. It is because of these identities that I feel I can relate to the emotions and reactions that the headscarf invites and to the different experiences of veiling that are presented in this collection.

Although this was a solo endeavor for almost three years, it could not have been completed without the commitment and collaboration of my sister, who enthusiastically stepped into her role as co-editor. Our goal with this anthology is not to provide the answer or uncover the truth. Each contributor shares the truth and it is these paradoxes of truth that we hope to convey. The veil is undoubtedly a controversial piece of cloth. It has many forms and functions, not all of which are related to religion. However, it is most often associated with Muslim women. As Western media outlets gloss over cultural diversity and portray Muslims as one monolithic nation (Eid, 2014), the veil becomes symbolic of "those people". The systematic "othering" of Muslim women is justified by highlighting the unjust cultural practices in those Muslim majority countries that either limit or completely eliminate the rights that were given to women in the early days of Islam. Although the oppression of women in many Muslim societies is a real concern that should not be overlooked, it is also important to consider that the singular narrative of the oppressed Muslim woman belittles the voices of those women who choose to cover and those who are fighting systemic oppression in its various global forms. Laws that ban different forms of veiling, such as the hijab and/or *niqab*, are becoming increasingly common in European countries. Such policies create additional tension between Muslims and the non-Muslim nations in which they live (Ajrouch, 2007). A recent foray into this controversy was the anti-burkini law in France that sparked numerous debates and provided fodder for satirical perspectives regarding the concept of acceptable beachwear. It also opened up discussion on freedom of dress and the patrolling of women's bodies, bringing these issues to the forefront of feminist discourse on covering.

Western secular feminists often oppose veiling by using campaigns that spark anger from Muslim feminists, who believe that their fight for gender equity is being hijacked by misguided attempts that demean the value that they place on the hijab. Western feminists have historically used the female body as a symbol of gender equality (Bordo, 2003), thus less clothing is equated with more freedom and improved gender rights (Pasha-Zaidi, 2015; Sheth, 2006). One example of this is the "Topless Jihad" led by the Ukrainian feminist group, Femen, in 2013 to protest Islamism in Tunisia. The protest did not go over well with Muslim women, who were outraged by the effort (Nagaran, 2013).

Recent discussions have revolved around different kinds of feminist discourse and the appropriation of cultural symbols by mainstream feminist movements. Women of colour have been speaking up about their unique feminist struggles – many of which fall at the intersection of race, religion, and gender (Davis, 2008). Whereas the secular feminist's fight for gender equality calls for equal access for men and women to socially-valued goods, services, and rewards (European Institute for Gender Equality, 2016), the goal of Islamic feminists is not necessarily that of gender equality, but rather gender equity (Bullock, 2002). Gender equity demands fairness between men and women – a concept that may apply more readily to the notion of complementary gender roles as reflected in Islam. With gender equity, men and women are expected to be treated with fairness "according to their respective needs and interests. This may include equal treatment or treatment that is different but considered equivalent in terms of rights, benefits, obligations and opportunities" (International Labor Office, 2007, p. 92). Veiling then becomes the intersection at which these two inherently different goals of feminist discourse collide. From the Western feminist point of view, veiling represents the oppression of femininity through the covering of the female body, whereas from the Islamic feminist perspective, it symbolizes freedom from the objectification of the female form (Bullock, 2002; Bullock, 2000).

The veil as a symbol of oppression stems in part from the attitudes cultivated during the colonial era when Eastern practices were promoted as both exotic and sensual while simultaneously being barbaric and foreign (Ahmed, 1992). Islamic dress codes began to gain popularity worldwide during the 1970s in response to the lingering influence of colonialism and Western notions of superiority. The rationale was often to regain a sense of power by reintroducing the cultural norms and values that were suppressed as a result of colonialism. By embracing traditions that had been systematically disparaged during the colonial era, the emergence of a visible Islamic identity in many countries symbolized a decolonization of ideals and a return to the cultural values of the region (El Guindi, 1999; Hoodfar, 1992). These global movements were prominent in Malaysia, Nigeria, and Egypt in the 1970s (O'connor & Khalid, 2011; Mahdi, 2009; Bullock, 2000), and in Turkey in the 1980s (Göle, 1996).

A visible Muslim appearance became increasingly popular in Western countries such as the United States during the 1990s when Muslim women began to shift away from Western norms of dress. This was and continues to be partly a response to Western secular feminism. It also entails the development of a religious identity as a way of dealing with the stress of acculturation that Muslim immigrants faced. For Muslims growing up in Western countries, there was continual pressure to maintain two identities, one Western identity for public consumption and one cultural minority identity which was expected in the home. The need to find oneself in the plethora of available and conflicting notions of "normal" facilitated a process of reflection wherein many Muslims embraced a religious identity that allowed them to have a voice that neither their home culture nor the mainstream culture provided (Ali, 2005).

This came to be even more relevant after the events of 9/11 when Islam and Muslims ruled the airwaves, becoming instantly linked with terrorism, any visible signs of the faith instilling fear among the general public. This prompted many Western Muslims to search for the meaning of their faith, to understand themselves and how the ideology of Islam was being used and misused for political gain. As a result, many Western Muslims underwent a religious renaissance after the 9/11 attacks, asserting their religion as a declared identity to strengthen their self-image and provide a positive counter-narrative to the negative one that purported to describe the "true Islam".

The "re-Islamization" of Muslim women after 9/11 made the hijab a symbol of the political struggle of Western Muslims, and raised the prestige of the women who chose to wear it, as they took on the role of ambassadors of the faith (Haddad, 2007). As Islamophobia continues to spread, the hijab becomes even more engrained as the symbol of Islam the world over. Although dress codes are mentioned in only two verses of the Quran, the importance of head cover for Muslim women has been described by some as the sixth pillar of Islam (the five pillars being the belief in one God and his Prophet, prayer, charity, fasting, and Hajj – the Islamic pilgrimage to Mecca). As a result, within Muslim communities, the hijab is often considered a litmus test of faith that is used to separate the "pious believing women" from the not-so-pious. It is not uncommon to find individuals and even community leaders who make comments regarding the lower status of Muslim women who do not wear the headscarf. Too often, a bareheaded Muslim woman is considered less of a Muslim (Hussein, 2007). "This view is reinforced by the media, Islamic associations and even the government when they turn to veiled women to speak on Muslim women's issues. The veil is assumed to give Muslim women the authority and credibility to speak on behalf of all Muslim women and Islam" (Akbarzadeh, 2010, p. 7). Notice the visuals that one sees in mainstream media. A Muslim woman wearing a headscarf is labeled a Muslim, but a Muslim woman not wearing a headscarf is usually labeled according to some other trait, such as her ethnicity, regardless of how much influence her faith may have on her identity. Unfortunately, these practices simplify, and perhaps even nullify, the diversity inherent in a global religious community that is comprised of over 1.6 billion people – a number that is expected to rise to 2.76 billion by 2050 (Pew Research Center, 2015)

Veiling has implied virtue since ancient times, long before the birth of Islam (*circa* 600AD). Veiling and the seclusion of women was practiced in ancient Mesopotamia, where the veil was a sign of respectability and status. In fact, the Assyrian codes of law that date back to 1000BC identified those women who were allowed to veil. As covering was a reflection of higher status, women who inhabited the lower rungs of society (slave girls, concubines and harlots, for example) were not allowed to veil and could face harsh penalties for doing so (Dossani, 2013; Ahmed, 1992). Jewish women may have also practiced some form of veiling, as Biblical evidence from Genesis (24:65) indicates, "And Rebekah lifted up her eyes and when she saw Isaac ... she took her veil and covered herself." However, it is not clear whether veils in Jewish tradition were related to the concept of modesty or to what extent veiling was a normative practice. Christianity also embraced veiling in its early days. The verse most often associated with Christian head cover is from Corinthians (11: 4-7):

> Any woman who prays with her head unveiled dishonours her head—it is the same as if her head were shaven. For if a woman will not veil herself, then she should cut off her hair, but if it is disgraceful for a woman to be shorn or shaven, let her wear a veil. For a man ought not to cover his head, since he is the image and glory of God; but woman is the glory of man.

Thus veiling was a known practice when Islam came into being as another branch of the Abrahamic tradition, following Judaism and Christianity. However, it became more pervasive during Ottoman rule when again veiling and the seclusion of women signified status and an exclusive upper-class lifestyle (Ahmed, 1992).

Islamic scholars have traditionally concluded that the headscarf is a necessary component of a Muslim woman's dress. Recent work by Muslim feminists and scholars, however, has attributed the requirement of a head cover to cultural and patriarchal interpretations of Islamic texts (Armstrong, 2007; Ahmed, 1992; Aslan; 2005; El Fadl, 2001). Whether one believes that head cover is mandatory, the ultimate goal that all Muslims can agree upon is that of modesty (Siraj, 2011). From an Islamic perspective, modesty is a code of conduct that not only includes one's dress, but encompasses the larger context of behaviour and human interaction. For example, Muslims are expected to be modest in speech. Speaking loudly, especially in anger, is considered a sign that the person does not have control over his or her behavior. Modesty, however, also applies in private because from a religious point of view, we are never truly alone. God is always with us or as the Quran (50:16) states: "And indeed We have created man, and We know whatever thoughts his inner self develops, and We are closer to him than (his) jugular vein". Thus modesty is a form of submission to God, which is the literal meaning of the term "Islam".

The concept of modesty and self-control is not unique to Islam. "The heart, not the hemline" is a saying that appears in Christian writings when discussing modesty and humility (Mahaney, 2008; Lebron, 2012). In the New Testament, Timothy 2:9-10 states "that women should adorn themselves in respectable apparel, with modesty and self-control, not with broided (braided) hair and gold or pearls or costly attire, but with what is proper for women who profess godliness—with good works". Thus, modesty is equated with godliness in Christianity as well as Islam.

Among many Muslim scholars, modesty is what differentiates human beings from other animals. Covering one's *awrah*, or intimate parts, is a necessary part of being human. Which parts of the body constitute the *awrah* is a much debated topic and certainly, a woman's *awrah* includes more of the body than a man's, but it is important to note that modesty is required of both male and female followers of Islam. In fact, the verse in the Quran which initially talks about modesty (24:30) commands this to men first: "Say to the believing men that: they should cast down their glances and guard their private parts (by being chaste). This is better for them." The verse then goes on to address women: "Say to the believing women that: they should cast down their glances and guard their private parts (by being chaste) and not display their beauty except what is apparent, and they should place their *khumur* over their bosoms and not display their beauty except to their husbands, their fathers, their husbands' fathers, their sons, their husbands' sons, their brothers, or their brothers' sons or their sisters' sons, or their women or the servants whom their right hands possess, or male servants free of physical needs, or small children who have no sense of the shame of sex, and that they should not strike their feet in order to draw attention to their hidden ornaments. And O you Believers, turn you all together towards Allah, that you may attain Bliss."

The debate over head cover essentially comes from the Arabic word, *khimr* (which is the singular of *khumur* as used above). A *khimr* is a scarf, which in the Pre-Islamic era was worn by women on their heads, but not necessarily covering their chests. "Commentators on the Quran repeatedly emphasize that women in Mecca and Medina were in the habit of exposing all or most of their chests, even if their hair was covered" (El Fadl, 2006, p. 197). The commandment, therefore, ordered believing women to use this fabric to cover their bosoms. Those who believe this commandment mandates head cover say that it is only logical in the context of the verse for Muslim women to cover their hair. After all, if a *khimr* was already used to cover the head, then why would God need to emphasize this point? From this perspective, it would be like telling someone that your shirt needs to cover your back! On the other hand, those who believe that head cover is not the primary mandate emphasize the idea that God does not specifically tell women to use the scarf to cover their heads. The commandment instead focuses on covering the chest area. According to this perspective, a scarf does not necessarily have to cover the head. That's what women did at the time, so it was a garment that was readily available but not necessarily being used in the most modest way.

Our intention in this collection is not to tell anyone what to believe. Both arguments have a point that is eloquently addressed in different ways by contributors to this anthology.

The second verse in the Quran that discusses modest dress is the following (33:59):" O Prophet, tell your wives and your daughters and the women of the believers to draw their cloaks close round them (when they go abroad). That will be better, so that they may be recognized and not annoyed. Allah is ever Forgiving, Merciful."

This verse was revealed in 627 AD, five years after the Prophet (Peace Be Upon Him) had migrated to Medina. Due to the increasing rights being given to women, such as the right to inherit, the men of the region were beginning to feel a loss of power, resulting in civil unrest. As such, Medina was becoming particularly dangerous, especially for women. "Muslim women, including the wives of the Prophet, were harassed regularly and required protection. When the Prophet inquired about the reasons for this increased harassment, he was informed that men believed the women on the streets to be slaves. In the culture of the time, this meant that they could be purchased, were sexually available, and toward whom sexual aggression was permitted" (Amer, 2014, p. 44). The verse therefore commanded women to wear their cloaks around them to be recognized as wives or daughters of the Prophet or as Muslim women, so that they may be protected.

In simple terms, this verse basically tells believing women to wear long, loose clothing so that they may be recognized as modest and not be harassed on the street. Even in this day and age, I can attest to the fact that in many parts of the world where I have personally travelled, it is less annoying and more comfortable (even if it is not necessarily safer) to wear clothing that fits these criteria. I emphasize this point about safety because in the current climate of Islamophobia, wearing the Islamic headscarf (or any head cover that may be presumed to be Islamic) actually *decreases* the likelihood of a woman's (or man's) safety in non-Muslim majority countries such as the United States (Cainkar, 2009; Amer, 2014). Even in Muslim majority countries, veiling does not necessarily prevent a woman from being harassed on the street.

However, it is not *being* safe, but rather *feeling* safe that perhaps should be emphasized. Feeling safe can encompass a larger frame of reference than just physical safety. For example, academia is currently dealing with the notion of "safe spaces" where students can express themselves without fear of being made unwelcome or uncomfortable. As such, safety is not just a physical concern, but also a psychological one. For many Muslim women who choose to veil, the physical form of the fabric can provide psychological protection by defining boundaries between men and women (Bullock, 2002; Droogsma, 2007). Women who wear hijab tend to have a more positive body image, so the veil can also offer psychological protection from media messages about beauty standards (Swami, Miah, Noorani, & Taylor, 2013).

It is important to note here that neither verse in the Quran discusses the specific nature of the dress that women are required to wear. It is unfortunate that many people refer to Arab dress or Afghani *burkas* as the norms of

15

"Islamic" clothing as this limited context negates the cultural experiences of other Muslims around the world. The increasing popularity of Islamic fashion can hopefully change these perceptions as head cover and modest designs begin to appear in branded catalogues and on runways around the world. In fact, the hijab made a grand appearance at New York Fashion Week in 2016 as a result of the creative endeavors of Anniesa Hasibuan, an Indonesian designer who had previously showcased her work at the Instanbul Modest Fashion Week. Such efforts open up the possibility of normalizing Muslim practices within non-Muslim contexts.

The headscarf is one form of veiling that is discussed in this anthology. Another even more controversial form of veiling is the *niqab*, or face veil. Islamic scholars generally agree that the *niqab* is not a mandatory component of dress for Muslim women. In the past, the seclusion of women – also known as *purdah* in the South Asian context — was considered a status symbol (McAleese, 2007; Haque, 2010). Today, as with the hijab, the face veil is worn for many reasons. Women who wear it may do so because it is their way of expressing their level of religious commitment; because they want to emulate the wives of the Prophet, who are considered, "Mothers of the believers"; or because it is in keeping with the cultural and/or legal requirements of the area of the world in which they reside.

The *niqab* is readily understood as a face veil, but the word "hijab" often communicates different concepts. Although the purpose of hijab is the practice of modesty as both a code of dress and a code of conduct, in general, the term "hijab" usually refers to the headscarf or veil accompanied by conservative clothing, such as long pants and loose skirts or dresses (Haddad, Smith, & Moore, 2006). In many cases you may notice that the terms "hijab", "headscarf", and "head cover" are used interchangeably, while in some essays in this book, the authors may differentiate between these expressions. This reflects the reality of the practice and the multiple ways in which the term is used in modern discourse.

In this collection, you will read some of the experiences that women have as they become visibly Muslim. Some women describe their journey to hijab through their personal connection with God. Others discuss it more as a reflection of their identity. Some wear it because they were inspired by a particular woman, while some people were encouraged by their family or friends. In the stories you read, you will get a glimpse into these journeys.

As our dress communicates a lot about who we are, it is also important to consider the experiences of people who interact with covered women. What do they think or feel or imagine? A woman in hijab or *niqab* may be saying one thing with her dress, but what is the message that is being received? Because there is so much noise and negativity about Muslim dress, I think many Muslims feel pressured to defend traditional Islamic norms. Our radar goes up and we fly into fight mode, ready to protect ourselves from the prejudice that we expect to receive. By understanding some of the ways in which the veil affects other people, we can hopefully continue the dialogue that is necessary for critical thinking and appreciation of human diversity.

And finally, it is important to hear the voices of Muslim women who choose to not wear the headscarf. Just as veiled women are subject to scrutiny, discrimination and pity in many non-Muslim contexts, unveiled women receive the brunt of the disparaging remarks, discrimination and pity in many Muslim contexts. The —isms in our own community need to be addressed if we are to work towards becoming an inclusive *Ummah* for future generations.

We organized the collection based on the themes that stood out to us. You may find as you read that there are other ideas that cross over from one section to the next. One of the goals of this anthology is to find the similarities that lie under the differences, so we hope that you are able to come up with other ways in which the essays could have been organized – other themes that you find which illustrate the similarities among the different experiences.

Given the relationship between veiling and the perception of "otherness" in Western societies (Ruby, 2006), we felt that it was important to look at the various ways in which veiling is perceived in different parts of the world. What is an oppressive practice in one context, for example, may be a symbol of female empowerment in another (Read & Bartkowski, 2000). We consciously chose to explore this phenomemon through a participatory action framework using personal narratives to guide the dialogue. A great deal of collaboration and discussion went into the writing of each narrative to maintain the authenticity of the voices while adhering to the structural and communicative requirements of the English language. As the contributors were ultimately responsible for their message, it was important to reflect on both their words and their intentions. Thus, the essays were drafted and re-drafted a number of times to ensure readability for international audiences. In many cases, foreign words and phrases were kept intact (aided by a glossary of terms) to allow for the nuances of the heritage culture and language to be communicated to bilingual readers (Lincoln & Gonzales y Gonzales, 2008). Interestingly, the foreign language elements were easier to address than the English colloquisms. English phrases and cultural contexts that were understood by some parties were sometimes incomprehensible to others!

By using a participatory action framework, this anthology is a conscious effort to decolonize research and examine the controversial topic of veiling from an approach that allows authentic experiences to be shared with an international audience. Decolonizing research is a relatively new way of approaching the process and entails cooperation between researchers and the people being studied in a attempt to lessen existing hierarchical power structures. In traditional research, the investigators are in a position of power. We define the area of enquiry. We collect data from people who serve as the subjects or perhaps more aptly, the objects of our research. We then interpret our results based on the existing literature and our understanding of the phenomena. Even in qualitative traditions, the crux of the responsibility for understanding the data lies with the researchers (Simonds & Christopher, 2013). With this collection, we wanted to do things differently.

As you read the essays, please bear in mind that the majority are not written by professional writers, but rather "regular" people from around the world. And for some, English is not their first language. By putting the contributors at the forefront, we specifically sought to include individuals who do not have as much access to the privileges of those in academic and media outlets. Our aim in doing so was to give a voice to perspectives that are often silenced due to a lack of access to the language and culture of the mainstream.

Part One, "Becoming Visible", discusses the challenges and the joys of those who have chosen to become visibly Muslim in the public sphere. Finding God and finding oneself are major themes in this section. Part Two, "The Distribution of Normal", discusses the dichotomous experience of veiling in Muslim and non-Muslim societies. This section highlights the complicated relationship between norms and personal appearance in different social contexts. Part Three, "Choices in Belonging", discusses head cover as a marker of group identity. Here you will find essays on the importance of belonging to a group and how the ways in which a person is treated by group members can affect the choices that are made. In Part Four, "A Lesser Muslim?", you will read about the experiences of Muslim women who do not wear the Islamic headscarf and the implications of this choice. Part Five, "The Pursuit of Sentience", is the final section of the anthology. Here, the essays discuss how veiling impacts the imagination and spirituality.

And so, we welcome you to explore hijab and veiling through the eyes of the women and men who have opened their minds and their hearts to give you a glimpse of their lives and their perspectives on this controversial topic. We hope this mirror on the veil helps you to reflect on your own experiences and ideas, and perhaps give you a reason to learn more about "others".

Assalamu'Alaykum
Peace be upon you

References

Ahmed, L. (1992). *Women and gender in Islam: Historical roots of a modern debate*. New Haven & London: Yale University Press.

Ajrouch, K. A. (2007). Global contexts and the veil: Muslim integration in the United States and France. *Sociology of Religion, 68* (3), 321-325.

Akbarzadeh, S. (2010). The challenge of being Muslim. In S. Akbarzadeh (Ed.), *Challenging identities: Muslim women in Australia* (pp. 1-7). Melbourne, Australia: Melbourne University Publishing.

Ali, S. (2005). Why here, why now? Young Muslim women Wearing hijab. *The Muslim World, 95*, 515-530.

Amer, S. (2014). *What is veiling?* Chapel Hill: University of North Carolina Press.

Armstrong, K. (2007). *Muhammad: A Prophet of our time*. New York: Harper Collins.

Aslan, R. (2005). *No god but God*. New York: Random House.

Bordo, S. (2003). *Unbearable weight: Feminism, western culture, and the body*. Berkeley: University of California Press.

Bullock, K. (2002). *Rethinking Muslim women and the veil: Challenging historical & modern stereotypes*. Herndon, VA: International Institute of Islamic Thought.

Bullock, K. (2000). Challenging the media representation of the veil: Contemporary Muslim women's re-veiling movement. *American Journal of Islamic Social Sciences, 17*(3), 22-53.

Cainkar, L. A. (2009). *Homeland insecurity: The Arab American and Muslim American experience after 9/11*. New York: Russell Sage Foundation.

Davis, K. (2008). Intersectionality as buzzword: A sociology of science perspective on what makes a feminist theory successful. *Feminist theory, 9*(1), 67-85.

Dossani, K. (2013). *Virtue and veiling: Perspectives from ancient to Abbasid times* (Masters thesis). San Jose State University, San Jose, California.

Droogsma, R. (2007). Redefining hijab: American Muslim women's standpoints on veiling. *Journal of Applied Communications Research, 35*(3), 294-319.

Eid, M. M. (2014). Perceptions about Muslims in Western societies. In Eid, M., & Karim, K. H. (eds.). *Re-Imagining the other: Culture, media, and Western-Muslim intersections* (pp. 99-119). New York: Palgrave Macmillan.

El Fadl, K. A. (2001). *And God knows the soldiers: The authoritative and authoritarian in Islamic discourses*. Lanham, MD: University Press of America.

El Fadl, K.A. (2006). *The search for beauty in Islam: A conference of the books*. Lanham, MD: Rowman and Littlefield.

El Guindi, F. (1999) *Veil: Modesty, privacy and resistance*. New York: Oxford University Press.

European Institute for Gender Equality. (2016). Concepts and definitions: Retrieved from **http://eige.europa.eu/gender-mainstreaming/ concepts-and-definitions**.

Göle, N (1996). *The forbidden modern: Civilization and veiling*. Ann Arbor: University of Michigan Press.

Haddad, Y. (2007). The post-9/11 hijab as icon. *Sociology of Religion, 68*(3), 253-267.

Haddad, Y. Smith, J., & I. Moore, K. M. (2006). *Muslim women in America*. New York: Oxford University Press.

Haque, R. (2010). Gender and the nexus of purdah culture in public policy. *South Asian Studies, 25* (2), 303-310.

Heibling, M. (2008). *Islamophobia in Switzerland: A new phenomenon or a new name for xenophobia?* Paper prepared for Annual Conference of the Midwest Political Science Association (MPSA), Chicago, April 3 — 6.

Hoodfar, H. (1992). The veil in their minds and on our heads: The persistence of colonial images of Muslim women. *Resources for Feminist Research, 22,* 5-18.

Hussein, S. (2007). The limits of force/choice discourses in discussing Muslim women's dress codes. *Transforming Cultures eJournal, 2*(1), 1-15. Retrieved from **http://epress.lib.uts.edu.au/journals/TfC.**

International Labor Office (2007). *ABC of women workers' rights and gender equality* (2nd ed). Geneva: International Labour Organization.

Lebron, R. E. (2012). *Searching for spiritual unity... Can there be common ground? A basic internet guide to forty world religions and spiritual practices.* Bloomington, IN: CrossBooks Publishing.

Lincoln, Y. S., & Gonzalez y González, E. M. G. (2008). The search for emerging decolonizing methodologies in qualitative research: Further strategies for liberatory and democratic inquiry. *Qualitative Inquiry, 14*(5), 784-805.

Mahaney, C. J. (2008). God, my heart, and clothes. In C. J. Mahaney (Ed.) *Worldliness: Resisting the seduction of A fallen world* (pp. 117-138). Wheaton, IL: Crossway Books.

Mahdi, H. (2009). *The hijab in Nigeria, the woman's body and the feminist private/public discourse.* Working Paper Number 09-003. Institute for the Study of Islamic Thought in Africa Working Paper Series. Evanston, IL: Northwestern University.

McAleese, M. K. M. (2007). Women in the Middle East, past and present. *Middle East Policy, 14*(4), 189-192.

Nagaran, C. (2013, April 11). Femen's obsession with nudity feeds a racist colonial feminism [Feminism opinion]. *The Guardian.* Retrieved from **https://www.theguardian.com/commentisfree/2013/apr/11/femen -nudity-racist-colonial-feminism.**

O'Connor, M. T. S., & Khalid, R. (2011) The hijab: Representation among the Muslim women in Malaysia. In *The International Academic Forum*. Osaka, Japan: The Second Asian Conference on Arts and Humanities.

Pasha-Zaidi, N. (2015). The Hijab Effect: An exploratory study of the influence of hijab and religiosity on perceived attractiveness of Muslim women in the United States and the United Arab Emirates. *Ethnicities, 15* (5). 742-758.

Pew Research Center (2015). The future of world religions: Population growth projects, 2010 – 2050. Washington, DC: Pew-Templeton Global Religious Futures Project.

Read, J. G., & Bartkowski, J. P. (2000). To veil or not to veil? A case study of identity negotiation among Muslim women in Austin, Texas. *Gender and Society, 14* (3), 395-417.

Ruby, T. F. (2006). Listening to the voices of hijab. *Women's Studies International Forum, 29*(1), 54-66.

Sheth, F. A. (2006). Unruly Muslim women and threats to liberal culture. *Peace Review: A Journal of Social Justice. 18*(4), 455-463.

Simonds, V. W., & Christopher, S. (2013). Adapting western research methods to indigenous ways of knowing. *American Journal of Public Health, 103*(12), 2185–2192.

Siraj, A. (2011). Meanings of modesty and the hijab amongst Muslim women in Glasgow, Scotland. *Gender, Place & Culture. 18*(6), 716-731.

Swami, V., Miah, J., Noorani, N., & Taylor, D. (2014). Is the hijab protective? An investigation of body image and related constructs among British Muslim women. *British Journal of Psychology, 105*, 352–363.

PART 1

BECOMING VISIBLE

Sabr

Zahra Cheema

> *"Patience is bitter, but its fruit is sweet."*
> ~Jean-Jacques Rousseau

I whispered, "Alhumdulillah, SubhanAllah, Allah-u-akbar" repeatedly.

Relaxing on the floor with my legs straight out in front of me, I finished my pre-dawn prayer. My mother sat just above me, shrouded in my grandmother's wide, white shawl, whispering herself.

"There are two problems," she said abruptly. "You wear *abayas*, and you're a woman."

She continued whispering, her thoughts clearly on something else. I continued reciting, and mentally braced myself for another variation of an oft-repeated lecture, in this case regarding the law firm I had recently started.

"From what I know, people don't want women for lawyers. And you'll probably only get the occasional Muslim client, who doesn't have much money," she continued whispering and ruminating. "I know if it was me, I wouldn't want a lawyer in an *abaya*."

My throat closed up, and I stared straight ahead. A familiar sinking feeling washed over me as the doubts crept back in. And then something else arose too, the feeling that it wasn't true — that it shouldn't be true.

"Marriage is the best option. You don't want to work, right?" She stared at me, gleaning rebellion from my lack of responsiveness. "It's best for you to just have children and stay at home. You'll ruin your beauty working so much. It's good to get an education, just in case. But you can't make that much money. Is what I'm saying correct? I'm just saying my own thoughts."

She stared at me, but I didn't say anything. I shrugged my shoulders.

When I'm in public I cover my hair with a scarf, usually referred to as hijab when worn by Muslim women. I also wear an *abaya* according to Islamic guidelines. I started wearing hijab during my second semester of college, and *abayas* soon thereafter, but my struggle with it began years before.

When I was a child, my dear cousin Sajjad married a lovely, young woman named Asma in Pakistan, both of whom would live with my family in the United States. When she first arrived, she was fascinating to me. She was witty, intelligent, funny, kind, and very beautiful. She was religious as well, and usually left the house with her face covered in *niqab*, in addition to covering her hair and body. Surprisingly, in pre-9/11 America, this elicited nothing more than curious stares. From a child's perspective, it only added to her already impressive aura. It was like being in an exclusive club, to be able to laugh at the occasional reaction from strangers, and be privy to knowledge they were unaware of. It was just cool to be Muslim, something to be proud of. What she wore was just another positive point to being already an amazing and dynamic person overall.

At the time, my own family was irreligious and gave heavy weight to Pakistani culture over religion. I was drawn to the small family that lived on the floor beneath us, simply because they were so well mannered, kind, and generous that it was like a breath of fresh air. They prayed, paid attention to small children, gave generously, laughed often, read Quran every day, and treated each other with kindness and love. For a child who was constantly exposed to the worst parts of Pakistani culture, it was like a revelation. They were passionate about Islam, and followed it to the letter. There was no contradiction between what they believed and what they did. It was truly life-altering to watch religion being followed without omission or personal preference involved. At the time, I wasn't aware that religion could be followed any other way.

One day, Sajjad left for the hospital, kissed his daughter and took leave of the family. He never came back. He had a brain tumor, went into a coma, and died soon thereafter. His widow vowed never to return to America, where there were just too many memories. I was ten at the time, and had just lost the best part of my life.

With the disappearance of the positive influence of the small family living below, there was a corresponding increase of negativity and fighting in my own family. My only refuge was in the many precious books that I had taken from the school, the library, or which were given to me by Asma — books she used to read when she was young. All of my free time was spent with my head in a book, usually lying in bed wrapped in a blanket. I developed a knack for tuning the whole world out. Always finding fault with any activity I engaged in, my older sister began complaining incessantly to my parents about my reading. I stepped into my basement one day to find my mother and my sister filling garbage bags with my precious books. No amount of crying could deter them. It was all I could do to save a few books given to me from Asma. The rest were gone. As I was deeply shy, I had only a few close friends. The rest of my time was spent alone with nothing to do.

Desperate for books to read, I started perusing the books that Sajjad had left behind. It was safe enough to read them — no one would throw out a dead man's books. Naturally, they were mostly religious books. I picked up the Quran and opened to a random page, and quickly closed it again. It wasn't easy to read, so I tried another book that was filled with easy short paragraphs. For the next eighteen months, I slowly made my way through a collection of short narrations about the Prophet Muhammad (peace be upon him) in a book called the *Bukhari Shareef*. I read each narration slowly, and thoughtfully. Noting an emphasis on praying, I found another book that taught how to pray. I memorized it and made a small effort to pray around once or twice a day, but never on weekends.

After making my way through the thousands of narrations in the *Bukhari Shareef*, I came to the conclusion that religion was too hard. Believing and respecting it was one thing, but doing it was a whole other thing. I might try following Islam one day, but in the interim I would just practice as much religion as I wanted, and I probably wouldn't ever go all in. I was twelve at the time. I loved learning about religion, however, and continued my study of it. I added *Saheeh Muslim* to the collection, along with a few other small books. I had regained some access to other secular books, and read them secretly at the same time. Eventually Ramadan rolled around and I had the vague intention of trying to pray five times a day during Ramadan, but certainly not after that. My first few days of praying five times a day went well. I decided to try reading the Quran again, it was the month of the Quran after all.

I finished praying in my room, and while sitting on the floor I grabbed the small English-translated Quran from my bed. Getting comfortable on the velvety prayer rug, I opened it up to a random page and started reading. I barely read two sentences when tears started falling down my face. By the time I had gotten to bottom of the page I couldn't see anymore, I was crying so hard. I blinked hard and wiped away the tears. I had to read more.

One thought filled my mind: "This is the truth." That one thought repeated itself over and over again while I read. It was like every wall came down and my heart was washed clean. I submitted myself to Islam that day as much as I could in belief, words, and actions. I never stopped praying after that moment, and never stopped striving towards perfecting my faith.

Yet, it never stops being hard. My first instinct was right — following religion is hard. But not because the religion itself is hard, rather, it is difficult to follow because others make it hard on you. Having always been a private person, I followed religion almost secretly. Yet, when others found out that I was suddenly "religious" the criticism poured in. Every flaw I had was made that much worse, because when a "religious" person is anything less than perfect it is tantamount to the cardinal sin of being a hypocrite. I could only imagine what would happen if I started visibly being Muslim by wearing the hijab!

I had submitted myself to Islam, but the gaping hole in my practice of Islam was that I wasn't wearing hijab. Not that I didn't want to, but it was just so scary. I didn't have Muslim friends. My family despised religious people, and I simply didn't know a single soul who wore it. I wasn't exactly the bravest, and I hated any sort of attention. Nonetheless, for years I wanted to wear it. There were days when I had every intention of wearing it. I would cry and pray to wear it. But when I left the house, my hair was blow dried and shiny. I wore makeup and my clothes were tight and fashionable.

I had almost given up when on New Year's day something incredible happened. I had asked Allah for a miracle. It was a prayer borne out of desperation, totally unrelated to my struggle with hijab. Although I can't go into detail, you must understand — what I had asked for was impossible. Impossible! Yet, in my hour of need, the impossible became possible. I was so grateful to Allah, and so humbled that I couldn't stand the idea of disobeying Allah because I was afraid of people. Hadn't it always been Allah that answered my prayers, provided for and protected me? That day I made the decision that, even if it meant losing everything, I would obey Allah, because He would take care of me if I did. I went into my room, covered my hair with a bright orange scarf and walked into my parents' bedroom.

"I'm wearing hijab now," I declared. It was like jumping into a pool of water without knowing how deep it was, or what lay below the surface.

Unsure of how to respond, my parents stared and said, "Okay."

I was seventeen.

In many ways hijab helped me find myself. I never lost any friends, if anything I gained many, but my parents never failed to see the potential shortcomings.

"Who would marry you?" they asked. "Men want only beautiful women, and you're covering all of your beauty."

"Who would hire you?"

"You will never get a high-paying job."

It's funny. Even after proving people wrong, over and over again, there are many who simply refuse to believe that a woman can succeed in the United States even if she looks different from the cultural norm. They continue to believe that a woman has nothing to offer but her looks. It still comes down to how much of the body is covered.

Now that I am a lawyer running a successful law firm, I can honestly say that being a "woman in an *abaya*" has helped me far more than it has hurt me. Judges and clients expect someone who is honest, compassionate, and intelligent, and they often show a respect for me that I can only credit to the way I follow the values in my religion. Small-minded people, however, can't see past clothing and gender to the person behind it. I know that when my parents express concern, it's a valid concern, because there are many small-minded people in the world. There's a risk to being a Muslim woman that simply should not exist in an egalitarian society.

By wearing hijab, you risk losing your job or not getting offered a position you are otherwise qualified for. You may be less appealing to a potential husband, less approachable to people who may otherwise be willing to start a friendship. You risk being treated like a pariah in a cultural climate of fear. As a visible Muslim woman, I know people might bother me. Perhaps I will lose clients who underestimate my abilities because they can't see beyond my clothing. I could even be the victim of a hate crime. But if the choice is between giving up a part of my faith out of fear of other people or taking the risk that makes me whole, I'll always choose to take that risk.

I firmly believe that it will be worth it.

Just a Piece of Cloth
Tanya Muneera Williams

"Regardless of hard times, my heart — it still shines,
In these dark days you're amazed how my tongue stays ablaze."
~Poetic Pilgrimage

For many, the hijab is just a piece of cloth.

It is a piece of cloth that invokes passionate responses in people all around the world. Some believe that Muslim women should be obliged to wear it while others believe that we should be obliged *not* to. For me, it is piece of cloth that embodies personal choice. I emphatically believe that the hijab, or what we call the hijab today, should be a matter of choice. I purposely use the term "what we call hijab", because in many circles today, hijab is less about material and more about modesty and conduct. And so, when it is worn, a multitude of reasons support that choice.

I realize that this sentiment may be far from the monotonous and homogenous stereotypes that fill our newspapers and television screens here in England and around the world. For those of you who are not familiar, these stereotypes include the idea that all women in hijab are beaten and bullied by the men in their family, or that women in hijab hate Western values and Western society. I shouldn't have to state this, but these are stereotypes and do not represent the reality for many women in hijab. However, I have come to understand that it is always better to state the obvious for the sake of clarity rather than assume that people understand the difference between stereotypes and individual experiences.

I am a Muslim woman. I am a rapper. And I do wear hijab.

Although I was not born Muslim, the idea of women covering their hair was not strange to me. I grew up in Bristol, a typical British city, characterized by its rainbow of cultures. The area where I lived had a healthy Jamaican community. Jamaica has diverse spiritual and political traditions, one of which is the Rastafarian movement. The Rastafarian religion is monotheistic and Abrahamic and the adherents are very thoughtful and conscious in their beliefs. In my local community and even in my family at that time, there were people who considered themselves to be Rastas and others who had a pan-African outlook. To them, women (and in some cases even men) covering their hair was seen as something sacred. Growing up, being covered was therefore equated with honor and respect. It was a symbol of modesty and seeking God.

A little closer to home, the form of Pentecostal Christianity that my grandmother practised meant that no man outside of her family could see her without a head covering. My mother also went to church, but the church where she belonged was not as keen to emphasize that particular practice. Nonetheless, as a child my mother rarely entered sacred spaces without a hat on her head. So when I converted to Islam it should not come as a surprise that the notion of wearing hijab was normal to me, although not always comfortable. I actually started wearing hijab before I officially became a Muslim. There was no transition period — on Friday I left university with a five-inch red Mohican hairstyle and on Monday I walked back into university with a green cotton thin hijab.

I converted to Islam just three weeks before the 7/7 London bombings. As a result, I felt first-hand how the fear of Islam infected the psyche of everyday fellow Britons. These fears were generally manifested on public transport and on the streets of England in the form of verbal and, occasionally, physical abuse, and the ones who were on the receiving end of this abuse were often hijab-wearing women. Muslim men had to deal with a whole host of other issues, but there was a significant rise in attacks on hijab-wearing women. So, one day I was a cool London chick, and the next I was "the wife of Bin Laden".

After the bombings, I was equated with a variety of presumed political ideologies, supposed affinities to terrorist cells and grassroots movements intent on imposing an Islamic Caliphate on British soil. It might have been easier for me to understand my experience had it just been this one single stream of constant misunderstanding. Instead, there were dichotomies that existed. Sometimes people would treat me like any other person and that was always refreshing. I would let down my guard and go about my life like everyone else. But then other times I was pitied, as if the hijab automatically made me an abused housewife who needed to be saved from her oppressed life. It also made me a foreigner in my own country. I can clearly remember the numerous times people assumed I was not an English speaker – something that didn't happen to me before the hijab. I found this assumption particularly ironic because I was an English teacher at the time! However, in the worst scenarios, I was actually abused and food was thrown at me.

As I was a new Muslim, there was not much expectation for me to wear a hijab at that time, but being the hard nut that I was, the more animosity that I received from people, the more determined I became to execute my right to wear whatever I wanted! On reflection, what inspired me to wear the scarf was not a deep spiritual connection to the Divine or His words. It was not the desire to continue the tradition of God-seeking women. Rather, the hijab was a form of protest and resistance to the growing Islamophobia I witnessed around me. It confirmed my solidarity with my Muslim sisters who did not let fear and hatred taint their expression of the faith.

Although I was proud of my political message against Islamophobia, as a hijab-wearing Muslim, I was not prepared for the feeling of isolation and the loss of femininity. This led me to question beauty ideals, race, culture and its natural connectedness to the notion of religion. I remember asking myself questions like, is there a Muslim hierarchy in terms of race? Will I have to compromise my culture or value system in order to be a Muslim? To be honest, I have not found all the answers to these questions, and so they continue to impact my inner dialogue.

I remember one particular incident in my early days as a Muslim that led me to promise myself that I would be true to my culture. Being new to Islam, I was keen to find out what London had to offer in terms of Islamic bookstores and hangouts. On this particular day, I was out with my best friend and bandmate, Sukina, who had converted at the same time as I had. We were wearing Islamic dresses that we had gotten from a Muslim sister we had recently met. This sister had told us that as believing women, such dresses were mandatory for us. I doubt we had ever been so covered in all our days of living! So, we walked into the Islamic bookstore in oversized dresses feeling like authentic Muslims. However, upon entering we were told that our oversize dresses should be black instead of dull green, and that my white shoes were showing too much flesh. And to think that we had been tripping over our feet all day in clothing that was suddenly not Islamic enough!

This way of thinking seemed to be popular among a number of Muslim women I met during that period. Modesty and piety were measured not by character or good deeds, but rather by the amount of cloth which covered the body. For those who followed this belief system, wearing the face veil put a sister at the top of the hierarchy and of course, less cloth signaled less piety. The more I thought about it, though, the more I became convinced that this attitude within the community was just religious materialism. I'm not suggesting that the face veil should be considered oppressive or exotic as Western feminists and media tend to portray it, but I think there needs to be more critical thinking and less judgment about women's appearance. Perhaps because I am in different circles now than when I began my journey as a Muslim — perhaps because I am a more confident in my identity and less impressionable — I think the idea of religious materialism is changing or at least that there are voices who are trying to find a balance between their piety and their physical appearance.

Photo courtesy of Tanya Muneera Williams

For the most part, I take pride in being a part of a worldwide community, a community in which, largely speaking, I can go to any major city and feel safe because I know someone who knows someone who can host me or at least who will be available if I should need them. And yet with this interconnectedness comes an isolation that is built on the diversity inherent in such a widespread community. Muslims are not a homogenous monolithic society. I don't think I can emphasize this enough! Our community includes a plethora of different cultures and their associated customs and norms. This is of course one of the most beautiful aspects of the Muslim community – anyone can be a Muslim. Your spirituality is not limited by your cultural background or any other socially-constructed demographic. Yet the vastness of the community can make it more difficult to navigate the diversity of ideals and cultural standards in which conflicting notions of beauty and expectations of women always seem to be at the forefront.

We cannot deny that we are living in a post-colonial era. The economic, political and cultural values of the UK continue to influence other countries, especially former colonies and protectorates. Muslim countries were not exempt from colonialism then, and they are not exempt from the remnants of the colonial project today. In many cases, resistance to colonial oppression came in the form of national identity and the emergence of nation states. Through this, a pan-Islamic identity became synonymous with a pan-Arab identity. However when thinking about the fact that the majority of Muslims are not Arab, questions naturally arise in regards to where everyone else fits in the spectrum. Aesthetics can play a huge role in shaping a person's sense of identity, on both a conscious and subconscious level. So what constitutes beauty?

As a British Muslim of Jamaican origin, my cultural norms and ideals of beauty are at times different from other cultures with a longer history of Islam and a form of colonialism that was specific to them. If I and other converts like me are not careful, our traditions and cultural concepts of beauty may fade away to European, Arab and, especially in England, to South Asian standards of beauty. Many converts to the religion feel somewhat accepted into the Muslim community – until they want to get married, and then the families are less inclined to let their sons or daughters marry a convert. The term "you are my brother but you can't marry my daughter" is used humorously to describe the hypocrisy that exists. This can lead to a feeling of belonging, but not really belonging.

I am sure some will think I am exaggerating or unnecessarily highlighting this aspect of our community, but I believe this is a problem that needs to be discussed without offence being taken, and without the people raising these questions being accused of having an inferiority complex or a chip on their shoulder. I don't want to stay silent on topics that may be uncomfortable within our community. I have seen too many women curse their hair in comparison to other cultures. I have seen too many women celebrate and praise others for the lightness of their skin. In the early days of my life as a Muslim, as I began to notice the layers of complications with culture and beauty, I learned that I was not considered physically beautiful by some. That was the only time that I felt like I wanted to take off my hijab. In fact, I came very close to it. My hijab was supposed to be a protection for me, but it made me the subject of curiosity (at best) and hatred (at worse) among non-Muslims. Although it helped show my allegiance with Muslims in the fight against Islamophobia, I felt that wearing the hijab also meant that I had silently agreed to the notion of Blackness as somehow being ugly or inferior.

As a result, I began to feel resentment towards Muslims. I started exerting my Blackness, my Jamaican-ness and my African-ness, which I mistakenly thought then were contrary to Islam. Through my own research and through meeting scholars like Shaykh Michael Mumisa, I started learning about the Islamic intellectual heritage of Africa and the historical heritage of the Caribbean. This helped me find my place in the Muslim community and opened my eyes to the fact that Islam had travelled the entire globe. This also led me to realize that the problem was a human problem among Muslims and not a theological problem with Islam.

In response to the whole "more cloth equals more piety" argument, and in response to hijab being demonized across Europe, whether through legislation, social attitudes or the media, many Muslims are doing maybe what we should have been doing a long time ago. We are showing the beauty of our religion by taking control of our narratives. This is something I celebrate! Yet with the boom of the hijabista movement (hijab-wearing women who are devoted to fashion), and hijabi fashion blogs, I am mindful of the difference between hijab in a traditional Islamic sense, and hijab as a fashion accessory, like a belt. But I get it — the need to craft an identity.

Being a rapper and a spoken artist, which is a performance-based poet, I have a unique platform from which to exert my passion and commitment to cultural diversity — not only through the actual music, or the spoken word, discourse and videos, but also through my style and clothing. The moment Sukina and I started rhyming as Muslims, we made a concerted effort to showcase our culture, be it Jamaican, British or harking back to our West African ancestry. Of course our hems were still long, just a lot more colourful, and we didn't trip on them as often! The ensemble was not always spot on. There were times we looked like a walking street festival and instead of uniting us with our audiences, our colorful combinations just made us stand out. But I can say now that I feel comfortable and confident as a hijab-wearing Muslim. My hijab encourages me to embrace spirituality and modesty. Not surprisingly, I have found that it is the people who hold on to the spiritual aspects of Islam that tend to be the ones who look past cultural notions of physical beauty.

Photo courtesy of Tanya Muneera Williams

My hijab is more than just a piece of cloth. It drives me to challenge injurious mind states within the Muslim community as much as it acts as a visible statement of defiance against Islamophobia. I live in London, one of the most metropolitan cities in the world. My hijab is often a conversation starter on public transport. I get so many compliments now. Strangely enough, random people often ask me for my advice, and some have said that I look trustworthy. But the real buzz for me is performing and connecting with the audience. In that moment, race, religion, gender — none of those matter. All that matters is that we are human beings unified through art and my hijab becomes a part of the music we share.

My Journey after the Hijab
Farhana N. Shah

> *"You must be the change you wish to see in the world."*
> ~Mahatma Gandhi

Growing up in the United States, the thought of "covering" or wearing the hijab never crossed my mind. My parents were conservative but they never forced me to think about it. I was always ambitious and strove to find a balance between my personal life and my professional goals. From the age of seven, I knew I wanted a lifestyle different from that of the stay-at-home Pakistani woman. As hackneyed as it sounds, I wanted to make a difference in the world, even something as small as a grain of salt. In the process I hoped to find my soul-mate. Unfortunately, while my dreams and ideas were modern, my parents were still traditional at heart.

I had an arranged marriage at the age of eighteen, right out of high school, to a man from Pakistan. Being an independent thinker, and strong in my convictions, I did not let this life-altering event discourage me, even though my husband and I had nothing in common. I attributed this to the fact that we had grown up in two vastly different countries and cultures. Growing up in the US had influenced my thought processes just as his views were influenced by his experiences growing up in Pakistan. Nonetheless, I performed my household duties and responsibilities like a good wife, while attending college and working full-time. He did his part as well, but I ended up doing more than my share, as is often the case with married women. The marriage continued for about twelve years, both of us working full time, and supporting ourselves, his parents and his siblings here in the United States.

My son was about seven years old when I began to really reflect on my life. I had just completed my graduate degree and was thinking about my next step. I feared that if I did not make a change in my personal life somehow, I would lose my son and myself in the process. This is when I began studying Islam, particularly the rôle and rights of women in Islam. I had never cried in my life as much as I did when I became enlightened of the mercy of Allah and the rights given to women in Islam. The pages of those books wrinkled and became brittle because of the constant tear drops that fell on them as I read. It was in 1998 that I decided I could no longer live my life as a hypocrite, married to a man with whom I shared so little. We had not connected on any level in the twelve years we had been married, and I did not foresee any change in the future. I thought the decision to separate from my husband would be the best for my son. I needed my son to be independent and strong.

After I separated, aside from taking care of my son and working full time, I spent most of my time learning about Islam and the rights of women. It was then that I began to think about "covering". The more I learned, the more the decision to cover sounded natural. I realized the commandment that came from God, while not explicit, made sense to me. The Quranic verse 24:31 in *Surah an-Nur* reads, "They shall not reveal any parts of their bodies, except that which is necessary. They shall cover their chests (with their *khimar*) and shall not relax...". People who are familiar with the history of pre-Islamic Arabia know that women wore head scarves even then. They tied their scarves (their *khimar*) on the back of their heads, leaving the chest area open. As they were already doing this, Allah's revelation to the Prophet was to tell his wives in particular and Muslim women in general to use the part of the scarf to cover their "bosoms" also.

In 1999, about a year after I separated from my husband, I made the decision to wear the hijab. I remember very explicitly that it was a Thursday night and I was in bed. Every night I would spend some time reflecting on my day and making my *duas* (prayers) before falling asleep. This night was special because I had decided that I was going to wear the headscarf from the next day. Why not? I already dressed conservatively, right? So I prayed. "Allah, I have decided to wear the hijab. I am not strong, so I may wear it in some places, but not everywhere. I am weak and I need your help. You say that if we do something with good intentions and ask for help, you promise to support us. So I need your help in this."

Before I explain the next set of events, it is important to note here that my mother and sisters-in law wore the hijab, and I had chosen not to. In the past, every time we went shopping or were out in public together, Muslims would say *salaam* to them, but not to me. *Salaam* is the greeting of peace Muslims say when meeting each other. It would irritate me that I would be left out of this tradition and my reaction would always be, "Don't they know I'm a Muslim too, since I'm with you guys?" I wanted to be seen, to be recognized as Muslim. I am not sure, but this may have been one factor in my decision.

The next morning I took my son to school. The office staff and the media specialist there knew me because I was a committee chairperson and active in the Parent Teacher Association. I remember wearing a floral dress and a cream-coloured scarf. As I walked in, people complimented me on my dress, but no one said anything about the scarf- as if it were a normal thing. I dropped my son off and was about to leave when the media specialist saw me and said, "Hi." Then, half-way to her destination, she turned around, came back, and added, "I should say *salaam* to you." Her husband was a Muslim, so she knew what that meant.

"Wow!" was my reaction as I left the school building. As I had to run some errands, I ended up at Target next. I recall walking in to the store just as a Muslim family was walking out. They had walked a few steps past me when the little girl let go of her father's hand, ran to me, and said, "**Assalamu' Alaykum.**" It was like a veil had been lifted. They could see me now. Even a little girl could recognize me as a Muslim.

It was at that very moment that I knew my fate was sealed. I had asked for Allah's help, and He had given it to me. There was no turning back. Standing outside that Target, I embraced my decision to wear the hijab as a personal triumph. Little did I know that Allah was preparing me for something bigger! As I learned more about my identity and began to trust Allah, I came to understand that my hijab wasn't just about me. I was beginning to understand the strength I possessed in being a Muslim woman.

Then, 9/11 happened. The towers burned and the aftermath threatened the peace that Islam brings to so many Muslims in America. In an effort to demystify Islam among non-Muslims and address the numerous questions that Americans had about our faith, community members at the local mosque recommended my name for a few outreach projects to discuss the rights of women in Islam. My first talks were given to members of a political club, a group of senior citizens, and the American Association of University Women. Never in my life had I thought that I would be a public speaker! And I certainly never expected to be speaking about Islam! Thankfully, the talks were successful as I did continuous in-depth research to make sure the information was authentic. It was after the initial lectures and discussions with non-Muslims that I realized why my decision to wear the hijab was so sudden and unexpected. *It was Divine intervention, so of course it was meant to be!*

In 2005, I was working as an educator for a public school system in Maryland. Outside of school, I was heavily involved in community efforts and stayed abreast of news post 9/11. Sadly, ignorance about Islam continued to be prevalent. Stories about Muslim students who endured bullying as a result of their faith were commonplace. It was at this time that I realized I needed to do something as an educator to provide teachers with authentic information on Muslim students and Islamic practices. Miraculously, I came upon a grant opportunity provided through the school system. As I read through the requirements, I realized the deadline had already passed. Not one to give up easily, I emailed the contact person and asked if I could still submit a proposal as I had just learned about the grant and my project was crucial to Muslim students everywhere. A few days later, they agreed.

My proposal was for a module which I called, "Overview of Islam for Educators". The essential premise was that religion and culture exert a powerful influence on teaching and learning. In an effort to help schools better understand their Muslim students, my project proposed to inform educators about the underlying principles of Islam as well as the traditions of different Islamic cultures. This would be done by providing instructional resources on the tenets of Islam and professional development opportunities to help teachers make positive accommodations for Muslim students in the classroom. I also planned to have a Muslim student speak to teachers about common issues that may be happening in their own schools and classrooms.

I was notified a few weeks later that the grant had been approved. For the next six months, I worked with a team of experts to create a workshop/training session that would be conducive to teachers' needs. Because I had never delivered diversity training to teachers, I was relieved that my first workshop was scheduled in my own school system. Teachers had to register for the course, and I was paid to not only write the module, but also facilitate the training. Although I faced a great learning curve at the time, the workshops were a huge success. I am proud to say that since 2007, I have delivered this training to educators in a number of states, including Florida and New Jersey, and through various organizations in Maryland.

Then in 2011, I was asked to do community outreach via video to Nepal and Thailand as a Speaker and Specialist through the US Department of State. The purpose was to talk about Islam in the US and how to establish an Islamic school. As a result of these talks, I was asked to visit communities and educators in Nepal to deliver training and lectures face to face. It was extraordinary and humbling to share my experience globally.

Training in Nepal
Photos courtesy of Farhana Shah

Back in the US, I continue to work as an educator in the public school system. In this context, hijab gives me the opportunity to not only provide information on Islam to non-Muslim staff that I work with, but it also helps me to connect with the Muslim students in the school. They often tell me that it is comforting to see "someone who looks like them" in the building. One student even comes to pray *Dhur* (the afternoon prayer) in my office daily. As I exchange Islamic greetings in the hallways, I realize that students who used to say "hi" are now comfortable saying "Assalamu'Alaykum," which means peace be upon you. Hijab gives me a voice that I never knew I had or needed in my life. I want these students to be strong in their Muslim identity and be able to advocate for themselves. I want them to be able to provide their teachers and peers with correct information about Islam to clarify the misconceptions that are unfortunately rampant in the media.

We travel through life thinking we make plans, but it is Allah who guides us through a "maze" to get us to where we need to be. Never did I think I would be teaching others about Islam, nor did I think I would ever wear the hijab. I know things happen for a reason, and as sensible as I am, I do believe in signs and miracles. My hijab has been instrumental in my journey as I grow into a stronger Muslim woman. It goes beyond a piece of cloth. It keeps me balanced between the secular and spiritual worlds.

Adventures in Hair and Hijab
Nadia Eldemerdash

> *"To exist is to change; to change is to mature;*
> *to mature is to create oneself endlessly."*
> ~Henri Bergson

The last thing I did before I left Dubai was get a haircut.

Well, not *the* last thing. One of the last things.

It was a calculated move. I had been living in Dubai for five years and had not been back to North America in about ten years. Now I was moving to Toronto and had no idea how I could get a haircut there.

"Women only" is a much more well-defined concept in the Middle East and in the Arabian Gulf in particular. The high school I attended in Riyadh, Saudi Arabia, was an all-girls school. No male teachers, no male staff, no males at all on campus. In fact, there was a large brick wall between our school and the boys' campus. So as you can imagine, a women's hair salon, at least in the Gulf, means female-only staff, opaque walls and doors that are firmly shut against male intrusion. This is important because it's the only way that as a hijabi woman – a woman who covers her hair as part of her Muslim faith – I can get a haircut in a salon.

Of course, you don't *have* to get your hair cut at a salon. My mom cuts her own hair, and for most of my life she cut my hair too. But an unfortunate incident involving a major layering fail – she essentially chopped it so that I ended up with one very short layer and one very long layer – and a rapidly upcoming wedding made me rethink my hair-at-home policy. There is a reason why haircutting is a profession, I concluded, and at eighteen it was about time I adopted a more professional look.

For a woman whose hair is covered to pretty much everyone except her immediate family and a few close friends (when you invite someone to come with you to the bathroom so you can show them your hair, it's the sign of a true and unbreakable bond developing), I am inexplicably concerned with the appearance of my hair. Several friends have pointed out, when I discussed my fears about getting highlights, that no one would witness any colouring catastrophes except me.

"But *I* won't be happy if my hair looks bad!" I would always protest.

What can I say? I'm a very vain person. I think hijab is a blessing in that sense – without it I would be completely obsessed with myself.

Anyway, I spent a year in Toronto, my hair growing out slowly. Then I moved to Las Vegas, Nevada. By this point my hair was at its longest to date, and while I was enjoying experimenting with it, I realized that this was not a viable long-term situation.

At first it was great. I moved to Las Vegas in September, and the cool dry weather tamed and flattened my hair, which is inordinately sensitive to any kind of humidity. In Toronto, particularly in the damp summer heat that I had just come from, my hair was constantly in a state of unruly, puffy expansion. Basically, unless it was in a bun, it was out of control. So when I first got to Las Vegas I was totally enamored with my suddenly well-behaved locks. I thought, "Hey, long hair is actually manageable now! Maybe I'll grow it out all the way to my waist!" thus I might fulfil my grandmother's long-held dream.

Alas, this was not to be. Sorry grandma!

It turns out that dry weather presents its own hair challenges, namely, dryness. With summer rolling around, I found myself repeatedly trimming dry, damaged ends. This was not something that I had ever experienced before, so I just assumed I had more split ends than usual, but when I was trimming the ends for the second time in a week I realized that not just the ends of my hair but large middle portions were equally dry. That was when I had to admit it: the long hair days were over.

One Friday at the mosque I struck up a conversation with a young girl sitting next to me. She looked like she was about my age so I asked her what she did in the way of hair care. She told me that a local beauty school did hair and that her mother, a hijabi, had her hair cut there. But when I called to ask if there was an enclosed space I could get my hair cut in, they said they didn't have anything like that. I asked around at a few other hair salons and even visited a few, but at each place it was the same story. Some places were quieter than others; some places had an all-female staff; some places had areas that were farther away from the entrance than others; but no place could offer a level of privacy I would be comfortable with.

45

So I did what every millennial does in times of need – I turned to the internet.

Ah, the internet! When every door is closed and the world has turned its back on you, the internet always comes through. YouTube has gazillions of videos about how to cut your own hair, with all sorts of tips on styling and layering and coloring. It also has a lot of irate hairdressers in the comments section imploring young women not to inflict such wounds upon themselves and come to their trusted local hair salon instead. There was also one particularly ungracious person who claimed to be happy that so many girls would follow this advice and "ruin" their hair.

After watching a few videos I felt sufficiently versed in the topic to attempt it on my own. About a week later I went to purchase hair-cutting scissors, which are apparently essential to such an endeavour, and found that you could in fact buy a complete hair cutting kit with a big bib thing they use at barbers' shops included. Armed with my internet knowledge and special tools, I then locked myself in my bathroom and went at it.

I think if I had to give advice to someone considering cutting their own hair, I would say to leave the bathroom door open. Closed, the room rapidly became warm and slightly damp and my hair immediately begin to puff and frizz. This is probably why, about halfway through, I decided I was sick of long hair forever and chopped off about four or five extra inches.

I would also suggest that you apply the same principles to hair-cutting that you do to other hands-on activities such as cooking — namely, watch your fingers. What I'm trying to say is that I snipped through my index finger. As you can imagine, it hurt a lot and it bled a lot. Nonetheless, I persevered so I can pass on the following lesson: be careful out there people! Hair-cutting scissors are sharp!

Another important thing to know when it comes to hair-cutting is when to stop. At some point you have to decide that yes, your ends *are* even, preferably within two or three hours after you first begin to cut your hair. I spent about two days after doing the deed examining my hair in the mirror and making what I felt were absolutely necessary adjustments to clearly mismatched sides, until I realized that I could not continue to "fix" this cut for the rest of my life. This is a realization that we must all come to, so my advice is to get to it early.

All in all, and after widely disseminating pictures to a trusted group of friends who assured me that yes, my hair looked *fine,* I really liked the way it turned out. It's also nice to know that, much like our pilgrim Founding Fathers and Mothers (who do you think cut their hair?), I can be a self-sufficient and independent adult.

More than that, it was actually a really fun experience, and one I may not have had if I didn't wear the hijab. How do I get this really cute, but sleeveless and see-through, t-shirt to work with my hijabi wardrobe? How do I project confidence and competence in the workplace knowing that I am "othered" by the hijab? How do I establish boundaries with male friends and colleagues in a firm but friendly way? How do I mark myself out, every day, when what I would really like to do is just blend into the crowd?

How do I get my hair cut?

I think that my life would be simpler, easier, if I did not wear the hijab. And sometimes I wish it were. But where's the fun in that? It's the little challenges that shape your identity and make you stronger for the big challenges that life will inevitably throw your way. So I say Hallelujah and Alhamdulillah for the hijab, for the ways it makes me feel – sometimes strong and confident, sometimes vulnerable and judged, sometimes restricted, sometimes freed, sometimes beautiful, other times not so much. And Alhamdulillah for the things it makes me do – work harder, get tougher, be friendlier, and do things my own way.

Metamorphosis: a Journey of Reflection and Change
Skifou F.

"Change your opinions, keep to your principles;
change your leaves, keep intact your roots."
~Victor Hugo

Metamorphosis is what I would call the transformation I went through over the course of a few years. I grew up in Morocco, a very liberal Muslim country where wearing a bikini and going to the beach were and are still the norm for most people. Foreigners often imagine Morocco as a country of desert herders and camel riders on account of the many tales that are set in the country and the movies that are filmed on location in the south. Morocco, however, is more than just a desert. In fact, the desert is the least inhabited part of the country; much of the cultural activity and diversity is found in the mountains, valleys and coastal towns.

My parents always lived off the coast. Four years after I was born, my family moved to a town just a few kilometres outside of Mehdyia Plage, an area known for its sand and surf. As a child, I remember being packed into a small car with my two older brothers, my sister and my four cousins, as we headed to the beach in Mehdyia. This kept us busy just about every day. When I was thirteen years old, my father constructed our first summer house in Mehdyia. From that year on, the summer house became our regular break-time destination. Weekends, short holidays, winter breaks and spring breaks were all spent there. So, of course that meant a great deal of time on the beach, swimming, sunbathing, playing football, volley ball, running, collecting seashells, walking and being with cousins and friends. During my high school and early university years, I spent even more time in Mehdyia. Many of my friends were sea-lovers and surfers, so going to Mehdyia became a regular routine. Often we would skip school and take public transport to spend the whole afternoon on the beach. During my younger days, shorts, miniskirts, crop tops and bikinis were my main items of clothing.

Things began to change, however, in my third year at the university. This was the late 1990s and many of my friends had started to leave town to study or work abroad in Europe or the United States. Having more time on my hands, I began watching television. This was the time when satellite TV was becoming very popular in Morocco and many of the accessible channels were broadcasting religious programming. Watching these programmes and reading about these topics made me reflect on my own religious practices. Although I was the first person in my family to start praying in 1989 and I had kept my Ramadan fasts since I was twelve years old, I never really thought about either of these aspects of my life. I used to fast because everybody around me fasted. I prayed because that was a way for me to communicate with God and ask favors from Him. As a result of my new-found interest in Islam, my discussions with my remaining university friends ceased to revolve around The Doors and Led Zeppelin. Instead, we started to talk about religion and the confusion we faced in understanding the differences between Islamic practices and cultural norms.

By the year 2000, most of my close friends had left Morocco, so I started spending my time with university acquaintances who shared similar interests in school subjects. My brother had promised to help me financially if ever I graduated with honours and got admission to a North American university, so I spent a lot of time studying to meet that goal. When I was not in class, I was hanging out with my classmates (Khawla, Salwa, Fayza, Nora and Kacem) with whom I had formed a study group. A lot of changes were taking place in Morocco at that time because of the growing influence of the internet and satellite television. People in general were becoming more aware of religious rights and duties as more channels were dedicated to understanding Islam. For my study group, that meant that whenever we took a break from reviewing the syntax of language or our phonology homework, our discussions revolved around our growing interest in our faith. This gave me the incentive to explore deeper. Religious practices like fasting, giving to the poor (known as *zakat* or *sadaqa*), and keeping strong family ties were things we did without actually thinking about the rationale behind them. Once I realized that Islamic practices are about spiritual growth as well as the well-being of society, they made more sense to me. One of my most powerful revelations was that Islam is a religion of emancipation for women. I know that this is not what many people think, but that's because our religion is too often used to promote personal and political agendas. As a result of my understanding of Islam, my views on life began to change. The metamorphosis had begun.

On a Monday morning, towards the end of April, some of my classmates and I were gathered in the hall before our eight o'clock class. A student that I did not recognize joined us.

"Good morning," she said cheerily.

Kacem, Nora and I were puzzled at first, but when she spoke, we recognized her. It was Fayza! She was wearing her usual clothes, but her hair was covered. As it was not winter, I couldn't see a reason for the cover. It struck me then that the hair cover was not the one you would wear during a Moroccan winter or the one you would wear because of a bad hair day. She had started wearing the headscarf for religious reasons. Two or three weeks later, Khawla and Salwa followed suit. At this point, I would like to point out that I am intentionally not using the word "hijab" here, but rather the word "headscarf". I will explain later my views on hijab as a dress code, but other than the addition of the headscarf and the longer sleeves on their blouses, the girls' attire hadn't changed much.

These events, however, triggered an onslaught of questions in my head – What was hijab? Did it refer to the same concept that my grandma used when she talked about her neighbour who almost never saw the outside world except from the small window on the roof of the house? Did it refer to the same concept as *Haik*, the traditional coverall that women used to wear (and some still do) in North Africa? Did it refer to the way of dressing that my grandma and mother used to follow? Was it a mandatory practice or was it just preferred? If it was mandatory, why did ninety per cent of the Muslim women around me not wear it?

I also wondered about the women that did cover. Did they cover for religious reasons or did they cover because that was how they were taught to dress when they were growing up? This was particularly puzzling for me as many of the covered women that I knew at the time did not even pray. If hijab was mandatory, when would girls or women have to start wearing it? What were the criteria for wearing it? Did it have to be like in Saudi where you couldn't show any part of your body and all your outer clothes had to be black? If you started wearing the scarf, was it a lifetime decision or was there a possibility of backtracking?

After graduation in July 2000, our little study group came to an end and we all went our separate ways. On 25 December of the same year, I left Morocco to continue my studies at Old Dominion University in Norfolk, Virginia. I anticipated that I would not be back to vacation in my country for at least two years and that I would not come back to live in Morocco after graduation. Because of all these life changes, my questions about hijab were left unanswered. At Old Dominion, between classes, daily chores and long hours at the library, I was busy most of the day. Once I got a part time job at the thrift store, I had very little time left for socializing. Whenever I was free, I would spend my time talking to a young Pakistani student I had met through a group of friends when I first moved to Norfolk. His name was Saad and we used to spend hours talking on the phone or Yahoo chat. Coming from a conservative Pakistani family which lived on the outskirts of Lahore, Saad was often shocked when I would tell him the things that my friends and I had done in school – the parties, movies, and late-night bonfires on the beach. He couldn't imagine life to be so liberal in a Muslim country. During these discussions many of my misconceptions about Islam were corrected. Saad was very knowledgeable about our religion, knowledge that he had acquired from studying the different schools of thought, the Quran and *Hadiths*.

Saad and I grew closer as the days went by. Although we came from different cultural backgrounds, our views on the future were quite similar. About six months after I had left Morocco, I called my mom to inform her that I was coming back in July to get married. Of course, she didn't know what to make of the news. What had happened to my education plans? What had happened to my long term plans of settling down in the US? How could I be sure that I was making the right decision? How could I leave everything I had in hand for a future with someone I had not known very long? Would I be able to live with someone from such a different background? After some discussion, Saad and I were able to answer all the concerns from our parents' side, but as we found out, it was more challenging to convince his family. The notion that their son would marry someone of his own choice and who was, above all, not a Pakistani was a difficult concept for a conservative Pakistani family to swallow. Nonetheless, on 10 August 2001, Saad and I were married in a very simple but traditional Moroccan ceremony.

While negotiations with my family were going on, Saad had secured a job in the United Arab Emirates, so that was going to be my destination after marriage. One of the things that Saad and I discussed while he was in Morocco for our wedding was the dress code in Abu Dhabi. I had heard stories about the reputation of Moroccan women in the Gulf. We were generally sexualised and relegated to low-class jobs that often entailed some not-so-honourable activities. I didn't want to be put into that category. We agreed that as I was moving to a conservative society, it would be better if my dress reflected the norms and expectations of the country. It was not very difficult for me to embrace this idea. Over the years, I had started considering hijab as a possibility after marriage. I had a number of Moroccan dresses made for the purpose of dressing conservatively in Abu Dhabi, but I soon realized that looking Moroccan might open me up to the unwary glances of strangers for whom the stereotypical Moroccan woman was a nail salon worker who knew how to have a good time. In order to avoid this, I decided to wear the headscarf.

With my new look, I left Casablanca for Abu Dhabi on a Gulf Air flight. Ironically, the date was 11 September 11 2001. That was the first time I had travelled to an Arab Muslim country. I wore a long, loose two-piece Moroccan dress called a *caftan and jellaba* with a small grey-and-black scarf that let bits of my hair peek through. I guess I was still not ready to fully cover my hair. One thought kept repeating itself in my mind: "Once I wear hijab, I have to be sure that's what I want and that I will not change my mind about it." For a month or so, I covered my hair only loosely when going out.

Back then, Abu Dhabi was not as open as it is now. There were a lot of foreigners, but they themselves dressed modestly. No miniskirts, crop tops, shorts or little black dresses were visible on the streets or in the malls. Slowly, I started to feel more comfortable in my new mode of dress. I even started to wear my headscarf so that it covered all of my hair. That's when I can say that I officially began to wear "hijab".

Let me explain here my definition of hijab. Based on my readings and understanding of the Quran and *Sunnah*, I define hijab as the act of wearing clothes that are not revealing in any way; clothes that cover all parts of the body except for the face, hands and feet; clothes that are not flashy, tight or transparent, and that include a headscarf that covers the hair and the neck.

When I ran out of Moroccan dresses, I began to wear *abayas* as a cover-all because these were readily available in Abu Dhabi. That was my attire for about two years, until I moved to Canada for graduate studies in 2002. The harsh winters and cold temperatures were not particularly conducive to wearing an *abaya*, so it was in Canada that I began wearing pants, sweaters and tunics. However, unlike my earlier time in the United States, my headscarf was a part of whatever ensemble I wore. Of course, this made me look different from everyone else, but I never felt uncomfortable. Many of my classmates felt curious about the way I dressed and would ask me about my faith. For some of them, that was their first time talking to a Muslim woman, so they had many questions. On public transport, I would sometimes get strange looks from people, but that didn't bother me. I knew their looks were a reflection of ignorance about a religion and a culture that were often depicted in the media as ruthless, inhumane and foreign.

In 2006, I came back to the Abu Dhabi. Money was getting tight so we considered taking up a job in Saudi because the pay was better. However, we were concerned about the lack of freedom for women in the country. We could not imagine ourselves living in a place where I wouldn't be able to go out by myself, without Saad as my escort. Alhamdulillah, we never had to make that decision as I was given a job offer to teach at one the leading private universities in Abu Dhabi.

Today, my style is that of the modern Muslim woman. I don't wear the black *abaya* any longer. I don't want to be covered in black from head to toe. It's just not me. I prefer colourful clothes that fit within the definition of hijab that I mentioned earlier. Now more than ever, I believe that wearing hijab has to come from an inner conviction. Otherwise, it either doesn't last or it causes unnecessary stress. All around me, I see women removing their hijab for a number of reasons. My cousin, for example, was pushed into wearing hijab by her husband. Later when she got divorced, she stopped wearing it because her hijab was based on outside pressure, not her own convictions. Many women in Moroccan cities wear conservative attire during the day in Ramadan but then in the evening they go back to their usual shorts, skirts and tops. Members of my family who live in the countryside always cover their hair, but this is not out of strong ties to religion. That's just how they were brought up. Women are supposed to cover when they leave the house.

Contrary to what many people may think, my hijab does not prevent me from enjoying my life. I still love the beach and the water, but now instead of wearing a skimpy bathing suit, I wear a burkini. I'm fortunate to live in the United Arab Emirates, where there are some women-only beaches as well as designated women-only days at the other beaches and water parks. A few months back, my university organized a trip to a beach resort in the northern part of the country. I had the chance to play volleyball after twenty years and that too in the pool! My hijab doesn't stop me from being who I am. It makes me who I am.

About a week after the resort trip, a colleague who had also been on the trip passed by my office. He greeted me as usual, and then added the following words: "My wife said that she has seen very few covered women who carry themselves with so much confidence."

I smiled and thought to myself, "Now that's a really nice compliment!"

Beautiful

Cassie (Nadiya) Madison

> *"The capacity to learn is a gift; the ability to learn is a skill;*
> *the willingness to learn is a choice."*
> ~Brian Herbert

I am a rather recent revert to Islam. I was raised Catholic in the United States. My religious heritage is Italian Catholic on my mother's side and Russian Jewish on my father's side, although most of my immediate family have become atheist. Growing up, I had Christian friends, Jewish friends, pagan friends, Hindu friends, and atheist friends, but I never had any Muslim friends. I had never even heard of Islam until I reached my teen years. I actually first learned about it in World History class. By that time, I had left Catholicism and become an atheist like the rest of my family. Catholicism didn't feel right. My soul felt empty, my heart heavy with sorrow and frustration. When I lost my faith in God, I developed depression and insomnia. Everything in the world was bad. I believed that religion was a tool of oppression and that it only brought harm to people. I believed that religion provided a shield for people to commit evil without consequence. I hated religion and I looked down on religious people because, in my eyes, I was enlightened.

What a fool I was! May Allah forgive my wrongdoings. I knew nothing.

Despite my hatred of religion in general, I never entertained the idea that Muslims were terrorists or bad people. In fact, I felt strangely drawn to Islam. "Why do my thoughts keep returning to Islam?" I wondered.

I was seventeen when I entered university. I was suicidal, depressed, and felt completely alone. I had decided that life was not worth living. Then Allah brought a man into my life. He was a good man — kind, caring, and patient. We began dating and soon fell in love. He was a Christian, and at first he kept trying to convert me to Christianity. I was unmoved by his pleas and arguments, for I had heard them all before. We often discussed religion. It was through these discussions that I introduced him to Islam. I was not a Muslim at the time. I just wanted to show him that Christianity wasn't the one true path, and that he was wrong to believe so. In my attempt to destroy his faith, I led him closer to

Allah. He reverted to Islam a year later.

Islam changed him. He was happier, more charitable, held more appreciation for life, more determination to succeed, and felt more hope for the future. I was shocked. How could this be? Could it really have been the will of Allah for him to become Muslim?

"No," I told myself. "There is no God. We created God."

So I mocked him. I challenged him. I relentlessly questioned him, trying to lead him to disbelief, but he remained steadfast. I was dumbfounded. So, I became even more interested in Islam. I wanted what he had. I wanted to feel what he felt. I researched. I read the Quran. I purchased a hijab so that I could wear it in solidarity with him, as his Christian family wholeheartedly disapproved of his reversion. I began to question him, not with the intent to argue and attack, but with the intent to understand. Islam answered questions I had always longed to resolve. I felt something stir in my heart.

In 2014, the two of us went to Moscow to study Russian. I was still an atheist, but it was during this time that I began to change my beliefs. One Muslim man I met in Russia truly amazed me. He was a Tajik man from a poor shepherding family. His family had fled from Afghanistan to neighbouring Tajikistan when he was five years old due to the threat of the Taliban. He had come to Moscow for an education and for work. He sent money home to his family whenever he could. When he was not delivering pizzas by foot, he was studying to become a lawyer. This man was an ex-neo-Nazi. In Tajikistan, he used to beat up people on the streets with his neo-Nazi gang. But then he started to practise Islam. He became a completely different person from the one he was three years ago. He was kind and gentle and he supported Jewish Tajiks, something that would never have been possible in his days before he chose to be a practicing Muslim.

These two men and their incredible transformations had a tremendous influence on my decision to revert. In Russia, I discovered parts of myself I never knew existed. I found the ability to believe again. I decided that I would try Islam for a while. I returned home for Christmas break and on 1 January 2015, I surrendered myself to Allah. Suddenly, everything changed. My insomnia vanished. I no longer felt alone. I was not suicidal anymore, because finally I had found a reason to live. I understood that the suffering and hardships I had gone through were tests from Allah. I knew that all my struggles could be overcome, because Allah never gives someone a burden too great to bear. I used to believe life was meaningless. Finding the love of Allah made me realize that life is wonderful, even though it can be extremely difficult and painful. I felt happy. I often cried from happiness while making *dua*. I never knew I could believe after seven years of radical atheism.

I celebrated World Hijab Day in the United States, right before going back to Russia. I had worn hijab in private before that, but on World Hijab Day, I wore my hijab outside for the first time. It was a lazy Sunday afternoon, and I only went out to a supermarket. I was very nervous at first, but nobody said anything. Probably some people gave me dirty looks, but I was too busy shopping to notice.

In Russia came the real test. At the beginning of February, we returned to Moscow. I put on my hijab, and I wore it every day. Although there are roughly two million Muslims in Moscow, hijab is banned in some places in Russia, and many Russians have negative views of Muslims because of the conflicts in Chechnya, Dagestan, and Afghanistan. Honestly, I was afraid I'd be assaulted. But Alhamdulillah, I was safe! A few people questioned me about it, and I happily explained to them why I had chosen to become Muslim and why I wore hijab. Some were satisfied with my answers and others were not. Those who were not satisfied were the ones clinging to the idea that Muslim women are oppressed and that Islam is evil. May Allah guide them to the straight path if He wills.

My reversion was a pretty big shock for everyone. I had been vocally, unashamedly, obnoxiously atheist. And then suddenly, I was a practising Muslim! I lost some friends because of it. They held such hatred in their hearts for religion, especially for Islam. It was sad. But I knew that even if I lost everything for the sake of Allah, I had everything in Him. I received some very positive responses from people as well. I made Muslim friends – finally – and they were so happy that I had reverted to Islam. Why wouldn't they be happy? For my Muslim friends, it was like a member of their family had come home after years of being lost. Many Christian and Jewish friends of mine were very happy for me as well. We are, after all, brothers and sisters in the Abrahamic tradition.

The most negative responses came from atheists, including those in my family. Of course I understood why. I used to think like them. They believed that I was moving backwards. They thought they knew what was best for me. It hurt me knowing that my family would receive eternal punishment for spitting in the face of their Creator, of the One who had showered them with countless blessings despite their disbelief. But I knew that I couldn't compel them to believe. I couldn't threaten them with a Hell they didn't believe in. I couldn't appeal to them about souls they didn't think they had. I could only lead them through my actions.

One of those actions is wearing hijab. I always loved the hijab and admired hijabis, ever since I first saw a woman in hijab walk past me on the street. I learned at that moment that a woman's clothing choices did not determine her worth, her beauty, or the extent of her freedom. True liberation requires confidence and self-respect. In my experience many supposedly "liberated" women are in actuality less liberated than many Muslim women. My sister, for example, is very concerned about her appearance. She agonizes over it every day. She spends hours every morning doing her hair and applying her makeup. She cries and refuses to leave the house if she thinks she looks too ugly. I, on the other hand, feel beautiful in my simplicity. I wear no make-up. I show no skin save for my face and hands. My hair is not visible. I don't look or dress like the women I see on television or in advertisements. I am happy with myself. I may not be attractive according to society's standards, but I feel beautiful. *InshaAllah*, one day I hope my sister can understand that.

Since wearing hijab, I have encountered a few people who are more forthright with their disapproval than others. In Moscow, I encountered a drunken man on the street who, among other things, accused me of wanting to bomb the Metro station. He was convinced I was an Iranian spy! I don't speak the language or have any Persian heritage, but to him I was an Iranian-American Muslim terrorist sent to destroy Russia. I was more annoyed and vaguely amused than hurt or offended. In New York, a man once yelled at me, "Go home! Go back to where you came from!" As a native New Yorker, this was more laughable than anything else. But, unfortunately, I can't always just laugh off the prejudices thrown at me. A few years ago, I heard my young cousin say that he just couldn't wait to grow up, so that he could "shoot all them Muslim terrorists". Children are hearing these things, and believing them. And it is a threat to everyone, Muslim and non-Muslim alike, for people to have these beliefs because they might just act on them.

People have also been nicer to me since I reverted and began wearing hijab. For example, one night I was eating dinner in the university cafeteria in Moscow. Russian food tends to be very heavy with pork, and this particular night there was nothing without pork in it. But the little old Christian lady who worked in the cafeteria identified me as a Muslim because of my hijab, and before I could say anything, she told me that she'd make a batch of chicken just so I could eat dinner that night! It was so heartwarming. Strangers now smile at me on the street and say hello, both Muslim and non-Muslim. I feel like they respect me more now that I respect my body and myself. They look at my face instead of at my body. I am a person, not a piece of meat. They ask for my opinions on important topics, because I feel they consider me an equal to them. My voice matters. They want to get to know me better. They see there's more to me than just what's on the surface.

I hope that I can change people's ideas about Islam through my actions, *inshaAllah*. I do a lot of art in my spare time, and lately my artwork has been for the purpose of *dawah*, educating others about my faith. I explain many things about Islam and combat misconceptions through my web comic, *Lessons in PEACE*. I have encountered people online spreading anti-Muslim hatred, and I explain to them from a Muslim's point of view why they're not quite right. And I've been met with positivity. Many people now look to me with questions, such as the status of women in Islam, the purpose of hijab, what Islam says about murder and terrorism, why people revert to Islam, and more. Some people have apologized for their anti-Muslim bigotry, or thanked me for clearing up their misunderstandings. As it turns out, most people who are Islamophobic don't know any Muslims. They only know what they've heard from the media. So when they actually get to talk to a Muslim, their ideas change. I have a friend who was a very convinced atheist, just like I was. I took him to the mosque for Friday prayers a month ago, hoping to open his mind to faith, and he's now looking into reverting to Islam, *Alhamdulillah*. Another once-atheist friend of mine just took his *shahada* after a year of talking with me about Islam.

I believe it's my duty as a Muslimah actively to speak out against anti-

Muslim speech. People believe that Muslim women are oppressed by an evil, patriarchal religion, especially when it comes to the issue of the hijab. This notion could not be further from the truth. My hijab is not a symbol of oppression. It is a symbol of my freedom from frivolous, unattainable beauty standards. It is a symbol of my faith in Allah, and of my joy in following Him. It is a symbol of Islam, a religion of peace and equality. My worth is not based on my looks. My heart matters. My deeds matter.

Hijabis are visible ambassadors of Islam. Wearing hijab helps me to control my temper, quiet my tongue if I want to say something nasty, and remember to be kind and charitable. It is a constant reminder that Allah's influence and guidance is with me always. We as Muslims have a responsibility to Allah, a responsibility to the *Ummah*, and a responsibility to the world. We must act in the way Allah has commanded. As hijabis, we are a reflection on Islam and on Allah.

It's been almost a year and a half since I became a Muslim. I still have depression, but I know now that I can get through whatever life may throw at me. The Christian-man-turned-Muslim and I are discussing the possibility of marriage. We hope to live our lives together in love and in worship of Allah. *InshaAllah* one day I would like to perform Hajj with the man I love. I realize now that my journey from atheism to Islam was Allah's will. Allah had never left me. I had never been alone. Though I had cursed Him, disbelieved, and turned others away from Him in my militant atheism, He had never forsaken me. He led me back to the straight path, and for this I am eternally grateful. Without the guidance of Allah, I would still be in the dark, but now I have seen the light.

And it is beautiful.

The Essence of Hijab

Maryam Nasser

"Modesty is the way you deal with beauty, not the way you avoid it."
~Tariq Ramadhan

Hijab is a term commonly heard and even more commonly misunderstood by a vast majority of the world's population, including Muslims themselves. Literally translated, hijab means a cover, curtain or screen, but in its actual sense, it refers to the demeanor and physical covering to which Muslims are expected to adhere as stipulated by the following verses of the Holy Quran: "And say to the believing men that they should lower their gaze and be modest. That is purer for them. Lo! Allah is aware of what they do. And say to the believing women that they should lower their gaze and guard their modesty; that they should not display their beauty and ornaments except what must ordinarily appear thereof; that they should draw their veils over their bosoms and not display their beauty except to their husbands, their fathers, their husbands' fathers, their sons, their husbands' sons, their brothers, or their brothers' sons or their sisters' sons, or their women or the servants whom their right hands possess, or male servants free of physical needs, or small children who have no sense of the shame of sex, and that they should not strike their feet in order to draw attention to their hidden ornaments. And O you who believe, turn you all together towards Allah, that you may attain Bliss" (Quran 24:30-31).

It is important to note here that, as stated by the verse, hijab isn't a concept restricted only to Muslim women. Rather, it must be practised by all believers. The verse also clarifies that hijab is not a choice, but is in fact a religious obligation incumbent upon every Muslim, male and female. Of course, no one has the right to impose hijab on another. Like all religious duties in Islam, it should be embraced willingly as part of our submission to God. "There is no compulsion in religion" (Quran 2:256). As such, Western misconceptions regarding hijab being a symbol of female oppression do not align with Islamic principles.

Hijab limits any unnecessary contact between men and women, and so concepts such as dating are contradictory within this belief system. The focal point of hijab is the maintenance of chastity to protect believers from unwanted sexual advances, so that we are acknowledged in society for our contributions, not for our physical appearances and beauty. As reflected by the verse itself, this is upheld more by practising modesty and "lowering one's gaze" as compared to the act of physical covering. It clearly mentions the different dimensions of hijab in order of their importance, which is one of the beauties of the Holy Quran as a book of guidance and mercy. Unfortunately, here is where the misconceptions regarding hijab begin. Most people regard hijab only as a physical covering which is to be upheld mainly by Muslim women. This belief is held by non-Muslims, and even more unfortunately, by Muslims as well. Yes, Muslim women are required to cover themselves more than men, but the philosophy behind covering remains the same for both men and women alike.

Hijab is also a test upon the believers, because it is no easy task to maintain the level of purity required by this philosophy. Muslims are regarded like pearls in their shell, where hijab is the oyster that protects the precious believer. The troubles people endure by delving deep into the oceans to find the most beautiful pearls just add to the pearls' intrinsic value, and in the same way, the trouble a person must take to understand the true beauty of hijabis makes them more precious as well. Such is the status of those who rightfully practice hijab, and it must never be undermined.

In terms of the practical application of hijab, individual Muslims and different Islamic sects have analyzed the verses differently. Although the majority of the Muslim population does uphold some level of physical covering, the details of this covering are hugely diverse. For men, it is compulsory to cover from the navel to the knees. For women, however, there are many different views in practice. There are some who believe in the *burka* or *niqab*, with which a woman's entire body is covered, leaving not an inch of skin visible. Others believe in modest covering that allows the hands and face to remain visible. Some do not mind letting a little hair show, leaving their necks open or wearing clothes that reveal their figure. There are lastly even those who do not practise hijab at all.

In my attempt to decipher the requirements of hijab from the verses of Chapter 24 of the Holy Quran, I have come to practise hijab in this sense: I believe in wearing a loose covering which disguises my figure, a headscarf that reaches down below my chest, allowing only my face and hands to be visible, and wearing a top that is at least below knee length. I usually wear an *abaya*. I don't wear makeup as a daily norm, and I ensure that any ornaments I wear (except the rings on my hands) are not apparent. Of course, hijab is more of an attitude than an attire, and so I maintain constant effort in practising modesty and lowering my gaze. Having the correct attitude is far more difficult than practising the covering. Maintaining a modest character is much more reflective of a person's heart than wearing modest dress. Unfortunately, this is where a lot of Muslims are lacking. Although hijab is a religious obligation, the sad truth is that many Muslims have not been taught the essence of hijab, which is why in many places it has become more of a cultural practice as opposed to a religious one. This makes it difficult to explain hijab to non-Muslims in any satisfactory manner. If I had to suggest one thing to the *Ummah* in this regard, it would be "if you've got it, please don't flaunt it." Being conservative in dress and behaviour helps one to focus on faith and spirituality by improving our self-worth and protecting us from lascivious gazes.

For me, observing hijab has been a pleasant experience and I've enjoyed each day that I have worn it. I have never felt restricted by it, nor have I ever been forced to wear it. Being a woman of Indian ethnicity, a conservative lifestyle is also a part of my culture. We believe that a girl reaches the coming of age (*buloogh*) at nine and boys at the age of fifteen, and that is when we start observing the hijab as an Islamic requirement. A girl can also reach *buloogh* when her period starts. Parents often begin to introduce the practice of hijab early in a child's life, even before we become *baaligh*, so as to allow for an easier transition to an Islamic lifestyle. In my case, I began wearing the hijab at the age of nine, and have been doing so ever since. I feel liberated by this covering, and I am proud of this practice that makes me so identifiably Muslim.

Hijab is a practical way of dressing, and it allows hijabis like me to carry out regular tasks with ease. It can make for in-depth deliberation when it comes to activities such as swimming and working out at a gym, as it is possible that in such circumstances one's hijab can be compromised. These challenges, however, can be met through the use of burkinis as swimwear, and frequenting of ladies only or mens only gyms. Personally, my hijab has not stopped me from experience sporting and outdoor activities. I have gone snorkelling in Zanzibar and horseback riding in my home-country of Tanzania. I've been rollerblading and bike riding. I have practised archery in Malaysia, ridden on roller coasters in various theme parks, and even explored the glorious Victoria Falls in Zimbabwe!

In Zanzibar (left) and Turkey (right).
Photos courtesy of Maryam Nasser

These days, I think a bigger challenge for hijabis lies in the increasing Islamophobia that restricts our daily movements in non-Muslim societies. I have been lucky enough to take many trips around the world with my family. Going to Muslim-majority countries has always been a treat because of the practice and acceptance of Islamic norms. I don't feel like an alien in public! Visiting non-Muslim parts of the world, however, can ignite a host of insecurities. I have seen how Muslims are depicted by Western media sources. We are often singled out for "random" security checks at airports and we get more than our fair share of unwarranted glares as we walk down the street. Even the general view that Westerners hold about the concept of hijab can be limiting. To have constantly to explain that my hijab is not a symbol of oppression can become tiring and cumbersome. I have to admit, this is probably the most difficult aspect of practising hijab, as it makes me self-conscious in public. It is ironic that Westerners want to liberate us from our hijab because, in reality, it is the irrational fear and skepticism that seem to emanate from non-Muslims in Western countries that limit my freedom.

On a trip to the US last July, I had hoped to visit a gun range with my father, as this is a popular sporting activity in the States. I've never seen a gun up close, but I figured it would be worth a try. I enjoy being adventurous! But as much as I had looked forward to it, I did have a creeping fear in the back of my mind that people in the US might react badly to me in a place like that. As it turns out, I never managed to make the trip to the gun range. The Charlie Hebdo attacks occurred while I was there and I was strongly urged not to do anything that would draw so much attention to me. I was quite disappointed, knowing that a person of a different ethnicity or religion would probably not have had to cancel her plans. Although I don't want other people's misconceptions of my faith to govern the way I live, I was grateful for the advice. Although it is unfortunate and unfair, I am painfully aware that when a few Muslims do something terrible in a Western country, all Muslims pay the price.

Emerging from the Chrysalis

Saadia Faruqi

> *"Verily, after every difficulty comes ease."*
> ~Holy Quran (94:5)

I look at my reflection in the mirror as I fix my hijab. No matter how hard I try, it looks off, lopsided. I tell myself the whole point of the hijab is to hide my beauty, to remove the ego from my heart. Who cares if it is not completely straight or creaseless? Sadly, although I've worn the hijab strictly for ten years and on and off for another six more, it is still difficult at times to accept. It's a piece of cloth, but it's also so much more. It's my best friend, and my arch enemy.

I think back to all the days we have seen together, my hijab and me. It was in college when I first stepped into its warm cover, although back then it was in the shape of a *dupatta*. I still don't remember why I did that, because nobody in my entire family or anyone I knew covered themselves. This was in Pakistan before the War of Terror changed Muslims to ideological apologetics, before hijab or *chador* or *burka* were fashionable words. So I try to remember as I stand in front of the mirror what made me first start this very unlikely practice.

Pakistan was, and has always been, a conundrum. Literally called "the land of the pure", it was born out of India in 1947 for the stated purpose of providing a country for Muslims to practise their faith without fear of persecution. Religion was expressed as being separated from state affairs, but it was never really possible. Eventually extremists won. As a result, much upheaval in the name of Islam has occurred in that country in the last fifty years or more.

I was born in 1976. Apart from political dramas and their extensive effects – the breaking off of East Pakistan which resulted in the creation of Bangladesh, the overthrow of a democratic government by a zealously religious Zia-ul-Haq, the official denunciation of the Ahmadiyya community as non-Muslims – the 1970s were quite alright in terms of safety, security and extremism. Many Pakistanis were Muslim in name only, although I suspect this was not a feature of Pakistan alone. They had a habit of turning to God in times of poverty or stress, and forgetting Him at all other times. Or perhaps that was my perception.

I grew up learning about Islam in school. Thankfully, as a Muslim country, Pakistan's educational curriculum included religious studies, otherwise I may not have even learned the basics of my faith. But hijab was not a topic of discussion during those times, in the classroom or outside. I saw only servants and other poor Pakistanis cover themselves, and it was more a sign of protection from the elements, including human elements, than anything else. So it was with me, not knowing or caring about this piece of cloth that would forever change my life later.

School life passed by without God. After ten years of schooling, students were expected to attend two years of college and then go on to a two-or three-year university. I followed the path well-trodden and arrived in college fresh and green, yet jaded in some ways. It was the early 1990s by that time, and things were changing in Pakistan. There was more crime, less respect for women and other disenfranchised groups. Early on I noticed that there was a lot of unwelcome male attention from bus drivers and chauffeurs and students standing expectantly outside my all-girls college. I remember noticing the girls who covered their hair. The catcalls and stares were never focused on them, only on us bare-headed ones. "Why?" I wondered, yet it was a simple question to answer. If I didn't want to be the recipient of male stares, maybe I should wear my *dupatta* over my head instead of leaving it dangling from one shoulder. I tried it, and it worked. My astonishment knew no bounds as this religio-cultural phenomenon unfolded in front of my eyes. I was hooked by the power of this flimsy piece of fabric.

I hid my new hijab practice as long as I could, covering only upon entering and leaving the college where those men lined the streets waiting for us. My parents would have been horrified if they had learned of my defection to the religious side. We were Muslims, but not really practising. We did some rituals, ignored others. They were both vehemently against the hijab, considering it a symptom of deeper societal ills, such as lack of education and enlightenment. I grew up hearing negative comments about women who wore the hijab, as if they were extremists and fundamentalists. In those times, perhaps that's what the hijab signified in Pakistan.

But I was adamant. I had found a certain peace and protection in this cloth that I hadn't found anywhere else. I have heard it said by many that covering oneself is the result of a high level of faith, but for me, at least, it was the opposite. I came to the hijab in a very round-about and perhaps even half-hearted way, but it was a force of its own. It led me towards people who were similar. Without realizing it, I began to pray more frequently, and the quality of my prayers improved significantly. Was it really the hijab, or my own yearnings? As I look back to those college years almost twenty years ago, I'm not really certain which came first, the chicken or the egg.

My religiosity was short-lived, at least the first time. I soon entered university, which was a whole different world. It was co-educational, and for the first time in my life I was studying, talking, laughing with boys. The opposite gender was no longer a nuisance, and the stares and catcalls were no longer unwelcome. That I forgot the hijab so easily in my attraction to a different lifestyle is a mark of sorrow for me now, yet I learned much about human nature from that fact alone.

University was an interesting experiment for me in more ways than one. It opened up my eyes to the way of the world and helped me realize that everyone who calls themselves Muslim isn't really *Muslim*. The institution I attended was élite and expensive. It felt as if everyone had coupled off, everyone appeared rich and fashionable. For about two years, I tried to find my place in this environment. Covering myself was far from my thoughts.

But slowly, the hijab reeled me back in. I became friendly with some hijabi girls in my class, and found a certain solace in their company that I didn't find elsewhere in the halls of the university. We talked about faith, we prayed together, we distanced ourselves from boys. Yet, straddling both worlds, I was not fully converted. The lure of that other, more desirable lifestyle still called to me. But I was learning more about being really Muslim just because of the hijab. I began fasting and praying *tahajjud* prayers, feeling myself coming closer to God as I struggled with relationships and grades in my final year of university. It was hugely cathartic and emotionally very tumultuous. I was at a breakthrough, though, and I knew it.

At home, things were not going too well with my family. I found it difficult to hide my growing religiosity, even though I never wore the *dupatta* on my head in front of my parents. But they saw me praying; they noticed the withdrawn attitude and became suspicious. I still remember the time my father stood outside the house as I came back from university, covered from head to toe. It was usually my practice to take off the hijab before entering the house, but that day he caught me at the end of the street, red-handed (or black-headed). The jig was up, as they say. I remember lots of shouting and threatening, but I was resolute: I wasn't going to take this off.

Everything changed for me that day. Some family members were sympathetic, others confused and even hostile. Nobody could understand how an educated young woman could throw away her prospects for a piece of cloth. I was called extremist, fanatic and crazy, but it didn't faze me a bit. Finally, I felt in control of my destiny. I felt as if I was living among disbelievers, and I wanted to escape. I imagined myself like the early companions of the Holy Prophet Muhammad, may peace and blessings be upon him, who were persecuted because of their faith. I felt as if I had no affinity for my own family any more. This religion of Islam was infinitely more beloved to me.

Some weeks later, against my parents' wishes, I accepted a marriage proposal. Thinking back, it seemed as if the hijab had superpowers — it cloaked me and made me brave, strong. I, who had never disobeyed my parents before, had now done it twice in the space of a few weeks. My husband-to-be was living in the United States and it seemed like a heaven-sent opportunity: the land of the brave and the free, where one could wear whatever one liked, worship however one chose. What a great reward for loving God!

But that land also became my second break from the hijab. In the United States, I completed my Bachelor's and then began working at a small non-profit organization. Struggling with a new husband, new life, new language and customs, I put my hijab away and began to enjoy what America had to offer. We went on road trips and visited many states together. We lived and loved and laughed. And the hijab waited for me in the closet, patient as always.

Then, 9/11 happened, and Muslims the world over became divided into two camps: those who became more devout, and those who tried to disassociate themselves from Islam altogether. Sometimes I think I became one of the latter group without even trying. I abandoned some of the praying and fasting habits of my past, but I still felt Muslim. I still communicated with God on a daily basis. Is it sufficient to be Muslim without the practice? And which practices and rituals are more important than others? It was a daily struggle for me, one in which I grappled with my conscience and swayed back and forth in my faith. Several years passed. My husband and I felt the absence of children and a stable life, but I refused to attribute it to my own actions. I felt as if God was unhappy with me, but I tried to force that thought out of my mind.

The warning bell sounded for me in the form of a Christian supervisor, who asked me innocently one day why I didn't wear the hijab like Muslim women she saw on television. The time and effort it took me to formulate a response made me realize I was yearning for it. I mumbled something about wearing it in Pakistan, about forgetting about it in the US — so many excuses to someone who didn't really care. Then I took a breath and really thought about it, and finally my answer was a clear indication to my own self: "My faith isn't strong enough yet." She found it fascinating that what she considered a sign of extremism was to me a sign of strong faith, but I had indeed found the hijab to be just that.

That conversation helped me realize many things about myself. I was astounded that I could have left my faith behind in Pakistan, whereas the reason for my migration had been to escape the taunts of my family. How did I let that happen? I also analyzed myself and realized that actually my faith was strong, or at least the kernels of it were still there in the recesses of my heart. I made it a priority to find my faith again, once and for all. I left my job, started a home-based company so that I could work away from men who constantly wanted to shake hands or hug or flirt. We got serious about children, and the prayers started in earnest again.

It is true that one gets closest to God in times of despair. It was almost seven years into my marriage and we had no offspring. I took out my hijab from the closet, dusted it off and wore it again. The prayer mat welcomed my tears as if they were old friends. I became depressed and then happy and then sad again, at this rollercoaster of a faith ride I had been on for more than a decade. Perhaps I needed misery to remain close to God, to my hijab. If that were the case, I welcomed the misery.

My husband and I initiated many changes in life during this time. We moved to Houston, which has a large and vibrant Islamic community. Being connected with other Muslims, visiting the mosque, praying and fasting in communion with others had a deep, lasting effect on me. I was reminded of my hijabi friends in university. Surely faith cannot survive in a vacuum – it requires nurturing and support. Our means increased, as if sensing our greater faith, and we bought a house close to a mosque. We started attending all five prayers there. We finally became *Muslims*.

And finally, God blessed us with a baby boy. We named him Mubashir, meaning bringer of good news. He was not just a baby but a sign of hope and acceptance from God. He was our miracle, and we needed him desperately for our religious survival. Still I remained worried. I could not get my past out of my mind. I constantly recalled my university days and the early years in the US and thought, if anything is worth punishing in the Hereafter, it is this. I sought forgiveness for my past life constantly, waking and sleeping. One day, in a dream I heard the words of Surah Al- Nasr of the Holy Quran: *innahu kaana tawwaba*. "Indeed He is ever-accepting of repentance."

That was my signal, the change in my life I had been waiting for. I forgot my pains, my past life, my indiscretions. I was a born-again Muslim, I had a resolve like never before. I was never going to let God down again, *inshaAllah*, God willing.

Much has happened since that dream more than a decade ago. I have a daughter, a successful career, I started writing and speaking about Islam. My family went through ups and downs that make up this thing called life. What we did do was stay true to Islam, remain connected to the mosque and I to the hijab. I wear a coat as well as the scarf now. So long after 9/11 I still feel the backlash, the discrimination, the Islamophobia that has become our burden to bear as Muslims. It is now my identity, the way people recognize me, and on most days it is a good thing. I don't always wear it with happiness, for sometimes knowing I will get stares and curses is more than I can handle. But I prefer to stay home on those days rather than go out with a naked head.

I never want to lose my faith again. Never.

A Million Scattered Pieces
Faizah Afzal Malik

> *"Two roads diverged in a wood, and I –*
> *I took the one less traveled by,*
> *And that has made all the difference."*
> ~Robert Frost

My decision to start wearing the hijab came after much consideration. Growing up it was not something many of the women in my family adopted. I wasn't even aware that the hijab was considered mandatory in Islam until I was an adult. As a teenager, I thought the casual draping of the scarf around some of the women's heads was part of our Pakistani cultural dress. It seemed many of the ladies would just quickly grab a scarf whenever the Quran was being recited and then shake it off again. I thought those who wore the scarf more tightly, not showing a single hair, were just more "traditional". Clearly I hadn't gotten the memo as I'd always liked to do my own thing and was too interested in writing, daydreaming and trying to find inner peace – yes, even as a teen – to absorb or fully engage in what was going on around me.

I was the outsider, even among my siblings. I often thought I must have been adopted because I had only notions of travelling and running away, as opposed to learning how to make the perfect *roti*. I think my siblings also wondered if my parents had picked up the right infant when leaving the hospital! Ironically it was a solo trip around Europe that led me closer to my quest to find my spiritual self. On that trip, I let go of materialistic ideals and, when I found myself in a dangerous situation, I prayed to the only God I knew with such fervour that I came to the realization that I believed in Him and I always had.

As an adult, I had many encounters with hijab-wearing women that served to dispel my previous notions of them. I had believed hijab to be against my feminist inclinations. It was for women who were obedient and somewhat coerced into covering their hair and beauty because men could not be held accountable for their actions. I was to be proven extremely wrong.

One spring, my husband and I stayed in Amsterdam with one of his relatives. A mother to two children, and a teacher by profession, she welcomed us into her beautiful home. She was delighted with the Swarovski vase I had decided on as a gift, as her husband excitedly pointed to the glass cabinet behind us, which was filled with crystal. I could tell she had very elegant and refined taste. I found it enchanting when she lit candles in the early morning for breakfast to create a romantic atmosphere for us to dine. Perhaps this was just normal to her, making an extra effort to add beautiful touches to everyday activities such as having a croissant and coffee. I instantly took to her warmth and was struck by the way she held herself with a certain grace. When I became agitated at something my husband had done one evening, I felt instantly comforted by her kindness and understanding.

It was only later that I was able to put my finger on what it was about her that impressed me so much. *She seemed so content.* I wasn't sure if it was the fact that I came from a family where drama was normal, but I definitely wondered where her serenity came from. In contrast, I was always on edge. I had always been more of a rebel than a lady, and as the outspoken one in my family, I had acquired a certain distaste for culture and tradition. I felt the need to express my individuality, which I often did through dyeing my hair red, blue and purple. In doing so, I was making a statement that I was not the average Asian/Muslim/girl or whatever it was I was protesting about at that moment. I didn't have children at the time, nor did I have earth-shattering responsibilities to stress over, and yet there I was, on edge and unhappy. I had a career I had worked hard for and loved. I had travelled and I felt I knew myself well. I had attained some level of happiness, yet on some days it became clear that I wasn't content, at least not in the way those mind, body and spirit gurus always spoke of.

So imagine my surprise when at bedtime as I was settling into the makeshift bed on the floor of her children's room, a magical creature with dazzling bright red hair popped her head in to check if I was okay. You may think that her red hair was a small thing, but to me it was a hidden sign; red was the colour I loved to dye my hair, the colour I identified with being rebellious, powerful and fearless. Most of all, it was just not what I had expected from a woman who wore hijab, which I'd always associated with antiquated tradition and culture. Suddenly I saw her for who she was — a woman no different from me, a woman with the same concerns and desires for beauty, individuality and self-expression. The difference was that she had made a choice to not let her outer appearance define her heart, her mind, and ultimately her faith. It's not just what you wear but how you carry yourself that's important. When she wore her hijab, she carried it with such grace and responsibility that, to me, it was a lesson in how to truly represent the spirit behind the hijab. This realization, as well as the sudden awareness of my own prejudices, made a great impact on me.

After I started wearing the hijab, many people assumed that I wore it to please my husband, yet when he came home one day to find me wearing hijab, he had no idea that I had finally reached that decision. He was just as surprised as the rest of my family! For someone who has always been so strong-willed, it irritated me that people did not see the huge personal decision it was for me, and most importantly, that it was my choice. I wore the hijab to please my Creator first and foremost, but also to identify as a Muslim, to try to be of that character that is part of hijab. Perhaps in a way I felt as though my outward appearance would start to influence my inward feeling. In some ways, it did. My level of faith soared and I felt more graceful and serene wearing my hijab. That's one of the things I think people who don't understand the hijab struggle with. The hijab is something that can be embraced, loved and worn with such happiness. The first time I wore it I felt as though my heart would burst with joy.

The final stage of my hijab journey was reading *Reclaim your Heart* by Yasmin Mogahed, during a particularly depressing time in my life. I was physically, emotionally and mentally in pain and I was looking for guidance, something to soothe my soul, and that's exactly what it did. It made me realize that my pain came from being too attached and expecting the kind of happiness in this life that we are only promised in *Jannah*. The book is not at all about hijab. It is about attachments and why people in this life let us down, because they are not perfect. Perfection is only to be attained in *Jannah*. The author makes the insightful point that if this life were perfect, what would the next life be called? So many words spoke to me, but fundamentally that book made me understand the reason I was feeling this pain. I was searching for my happiness in the wrong place. I was being disappointed time and again, both by those closest to me as well as those who were practically strangers, because I felt everything too deeply, and I expected the kind of perfection from people that they could never give me. I still remind myself of this every day because it is human nature to try to "find" happiness and inner peace. Through articles, movies, quotes on Pinterest, advertisements and events, this world urges us to seek happiness, to take control of it. Reading Yasmin's words, it was as if everything I'd ever been told about Islam suddenly made sense, as if a million scattered pieces all came together perfectly. I finally understood myself. I just "got it".

I was blessed to have been with someone at that time who I knew would support me in my decision to wear hijab. It was he who had been the one to ask me many years ago if I knew hijab was mandatory in Islam and that he only wanted me to be aware of this requirement as he wanted to be with me, not just in this life but in *Jannah* as well. Love in *Jannah* is everlasting. There is no separation and no end. Whilst we did not get our forever in this life, I have never forgotten the words that he said to me with such sincerity. I have wondered many times, if he had been the kind of man who wanted to show me off in this world, without a care for my soul, would I have made a different choice later on? I hope not. Wearing the hijab must be accompanied with the sincere intention to wear it for the sake of the Creator. The misguided men who force their wives, daughters and sisters into wearing hijab are not doing them any favours, unless these women find the spiritual and other benefits from observing hijab of their own free will and come to love it themselves.

I committed to wearing hijab full time over one New Year's holiday. Although I was secure in my decision, I experienced a restless night before going to work, knowing that I would be the only hijab wearing woman at the publishing company I then worked at. I worried about how people would react. I knew that some people would have prejudices as I had had in the past. Even those who did not hold negative biases would nonetheless want to understand the reasons behind my very personal decision. Ultimately, as I stepped into the exposed atrium the next morning, openly displaying a part of my life that had until then remained private, I felt exhilarated despite my nerves. Spurred on by the encouraging messages from friends who told me how "brave" my decision was, I felt like the rebel I had always been.

Today and every day since I began wearing the hijab, I say to the world: I don't care who you want me to be. I choose the way I dress and identify and express myself, and I will not be judged for the way I look. Instead I will be judged for my intellect, my grace, my quirks, my individuality, my heart, and my faith because, for me, those are the aspects that I want to be considered. It is my soul that matters, not the body in which it resides.

A Covered Racer
Aida Othman

"Out on the roads there is fitness and self-discovery
and the persons we were destined to be."
~Dr. George Sheehan

Religion is a way of life for me. So is sport. I have always been a runner — something I was good at in primary school and secondary school, growing up as an ethnic Malay in Malaysia. During my adolescent years, a sporty lifestyle did not seem compatible with my decision to wear hijab, so for many years I put aside my love of running and turned my focus towards academic work and religion. But sport remained a part of me.

My journey to becoming a hijabi was interesting because I was not raised in a family that required it. When I was a child, I wore hijab only in the evenings when I attended an Islamic school. I was really introduced to the idea of wearing hijab regularly at the age of sixteen. I was at boarding school and I decided to cover my hair during Ramadan in an effort to respect the holy month. The experience helped me develop a better understanding of the reasons why hijab is considered a divine Islamic law for women. It was this understanding that inspired me fully to embrace the head covering when I turned eighteen.

That was also the year I moved to Auckland, New Zealand, to pursue my tertiary education. I received a scholarship from a Malaysian trustee organization to pursue a foundation year in high school and four years of university abroad. It was not easy wearing hijab in a Western society, especially in a post-9/11 world. It was particularly challenging when I obtained my first job after graduation. However, with patience and discipline, observing hijab became a way of life. Living in New Zealand was also helpful in encouraging me to become steadfast in my beliefs. Choice of clothing and religious practice in New Zealand is considered a human right, which allows for the freedom to dress in a manner fitting with the devotional observance of any religion.

Despite that, I did struggle at times. Beach culture is very popular during the hot summer months in New Zealand, and I was not confident nor entirely sure how to be covered in my early days in Auckland in order to enjoy beach life. In

Islam, hijab is mandated to protect and dignify a woman's status in public. It is not just for adornment but rather a way of promoting modesty. Aside from the face and hands, Muslim women are not supposed to expose their bodies. I have actually received a lot of praise and respect from non-Muslims about my decision to maintain hijab in a Western society where too often the media glamourizes and sexualizes certain body images for women. My decision enabled me to reject those images and dress in a more modest fashion that dignified and protected me from some of these unnecessary and harmful social issues

However, figuring out what to wear to the beach or how to express my sporty side was a challenge. That's when I got the idea to start wearing Buff – a tubular hat that sports enthusiasts wrap around their heads to draw off sweat and protect against sun and wind. For me, the light-weight material could also serve as a hijab, allowing me to accommodate both my religious beliefs and my love of sports. Once I made the discovery, exercising at the local gym and running on the pavement in Auckland became a regular routine. This was a turning point as I began to allocate time outside my busy work schedule to put some effort into exercise and fitness.

From my start as a leisure runner, I was able to take up running as a competitive sport after many years. I ran my first half-marathon in Sydney in 2007. My running career blossomed as I competed in a full marathon for the first time in Prague in 2012 and then an ultra-marathon in Spain in 2013. I have a collection of hijab that I wear while running, depending on whether I'm participating in a short distance run, a marathon or an ultra-distance competition. I vary my hijab based on the style of race and the weather of the location where the event is being held.

These days I have embraced my sporty side again, feeling confident and comfortable in my skin and my attire. As an experienced hijab wearer, I have no problems going from a pool, to a run, to a yoga session, followed by a lunch with friends and a trip to the mosque for prayer — all in one go. I no longer feel awkward. Wearing hijab is an integral part of my life and I enjoy experimenting with different styles and fabrics that are light and breathable, but also compliant with my religious beliefs. Being true to my religion and my love of sports has opened up different opportunities for me. As a fan of the

Islamic-compliant headgear company Capsters, I was honoured to appear as their brand role model to publicize hijabi sports gear. I was also recently a guest speaker at the 2015 Malaysian Women's Marathon.

Prague Marathon, 2012.
Photo courtesy of Aida Othman

Now that I live in the United Arab Emirates, I try to encourage other Muslim women to participate in outdoor sports, even if they cover themselves. When I'm asked how I handle the heat while running, I explain that it is about mind over matter. I advise other Muslim women interested in running on what the best clothes are for them to be able to participate comfortably in the sport. At a boot camp here in Dubai, I trained in Ramadan during the summer after *iftar* (breaking fasting). When newbies complained about how hot they were or how they were ready to quit during the boot camp, all they would have to do is look at me sweating and fully covered, then they would continue to exercise, knowing that they had to raise the bar.

Many of my friends look at me and they are impressed with how active I am in sports and outdoor activities. One close friend said I am the most active hijabi that she knows of. A British friend, who shares my love of running, said that because I ran for twelve days as part of a fundraising campaign in the UAE for two consecutive years (called 7 EmiratesRun), I defied all limits. And a Dutch male runner friend said that I am an example of a Muslim woman who is far from being oppressed, which is often the impression that governments or academics or intellectuals try to give when justifying their criticism of hijab.

Desert Run, 2014, UAE
Photo courtesy of Aida Othman

Unfortunately, such criticisms promote an incorrect perception. Hijab is never oppressive when it is based on correct teaching and understanding of its practicality and reasoning under Islamic law. As with any aspect of the religion, there is no compulsion to practice hijab. Neither is it necessary or sufficient to measure piety. Rather, believing women consider it a personal choice to show the level of faith one has towards Allah. Wearing hijab is a part of my personal journey towards excellence as I strive to become a better Muslim. It is a personal transformation for me to be a better person both inwardly and outwardly. There is a level of creativity involved with hijab as I seek to use my head covering to reflect my own personal style. Wearing hijab also gives me the opportunity to engage in an open dialogue with others and serve as a strong role model within our community to eradicate the negative perceptions and prejudice that society has towards Muslim women wearing hijab.

I appreciate when people see all that I have achieved and how I use sports to help my community rather than focusing on what I wear or what I have on my head. Hijab has never limited me. In fact, it has empowered me as a Muslim woman and it is empowering for Muslim women like me. It not only protects me and gives me modesty; it also provides me with a sense of liberty, individuality and uniqueness. It has opened up the world for me.

Ultra Trail du Mont Blanc CCC, 2015
Photo courtesy of Aida Othman

In August 2015, I was honored to qualify and participate in the prestigious Ultra Trail du Mont Blanc CCC race, which starts in Courmayeur, Italy and goes through Champex, Switzerland before finishing in Chamonix, France. The race involves a challenging run circumambulating Europe's highest peak, Mont Blanc. Participants must run and climb a distance of 101 kilometers (almost 63 miles), rising to an elevation of 6000 meters (nearly 20,000 feet) within 26 hours.

I reached the first summit where the view was breathtaking. There was an amazing atmosphere in Courmayeur as cowbells rang and locals shouted "Bravo" to cheer on the runners. But the challenging environment and the heat proved too much this time around, so I had to withdraw from the race along with over six hundred other runners The mountain experience was humbling and taught me many lessons as a runner and a human being. One can never give up, but instead get up and continue. So I will be back *inshaAllah*. I will train harder to realize this dream and chase the unfinished business of tackling this race. The mountain was too strong that day, but the willpower to come back is even stronger.

Letters from the Re-Jabi

Zehra Naqvi

> *"You can't make up anything anymore. The world itself is a satire.*
> *All you're doing is recording it."*
> ~Art Buchwald

Dear Stranger with a Chip on Shoulder/Saviour/Feminist Friend,

I'm an attorney, a community organizer, and writer. Interestingly enough, all those things are about appreciating nuance. I make a living by reading between the lines, writing the lines, and adding context to the lines. I'm also quite well-travelled and have friends from all sorts of backgrounds. I'm well read. I'm a perpetual student of the world and history and movements. So, if you're going to talk down to me, come ready. I bore easily and bear sarcasm as a weapon.

Me wearing a head covering? Not oppression. I am making the *choice* to wear it in a country that was founded on *religious freedom*. No one is making me wear it. I don't care whether others wear it or not. I don't think that wearing/not wearing a head covering will determine whether someone's going to heaven or hell. My understanding of God is that He is less Anna Wintour and more about big picture things like how we treat each other as human beings. I don't think people should be forced to wear it. Did you decide how to dress yourself today? Cool, so did I. I like wearing it, I like how I feel wearing it, so I wear it.

And just to be clear, I'm not assuming responsibility for the action of men. The concept of hijab requires men to observe modesty as well. Not just in their clothing, but in how they treat women. If men are acting badly, it's not Islam that's to blame. They're running afoul of Islam if they're engaging in any form of sexual harassment, assault, etc. That's not on any woman. It's every soul for itself that will have to account to God.

Did you just say I should go back home? I'm actually being super American by standing by my religious beliefs. You're actually being a total fascist, trying to impose *your* viewpoint on me. You hate ISIS? Yeah, I do too. You know what ISIS does? *They try to impose their viewpoints on others.* Careful you don't become what you hate.

So, basically, can you go save someone who actually needs saving? Or can you direct your efforts to rolling back racial and faith-based profiling, which is actually oppressive to me? Hello? Hey! Where did you go? Typical...

Best,
Zehra

Dear Pizza Place Guys,

I want to apologize for not giving you the benefit of the doubt. I just started working in the neighbourhood and I was hunting for a good pizza place. I came in and you looked at me pretty intensely. I was thinking, great, here we go. I assumed the worst.

I placed my order and reached the register, where you were waiting. You abruptly said to me, "We don't sell *burka* here." I sighed, nodded and put my guard up. You repeated, "You understand, we don't sell BURKA here." I said, "Yes, okay," but then you must have sensed I wasn't understanding you because you repeated, "Bork! BORK!" And I asked, "Bork? Oh, are you saying pork?" "Yes, that's what I said, no bork!" And I thanked you for letting me know.

Also, weeks later, when I came by, I was waiting behind a big, intimidating looking guy who was giving me a dirty look. Can I just say that I loved that. as soon as you saw me, you smiled and said, "Assalamu'Alaykum" loudly and proudly while you rang his order up? That guy didn't know what to do. He was outnumbered.

Best,
Zehra

Dear Woman on the Train,

OMG, do I have something on my face? In my teeth? Oh! You're staring at me because I'm wearing a head scarf. As it's technically wrapped around my head but out of my sight line, I sometimes forget that I'm wearing it. So when you're staring at me, it takes me a second to understand why.

But then I see you staring at me. Like a lot. Like your eyes are going to pop out of their sockets. You are making it very clear that you're judging me. I choose to smile at you. That's my first response. But, I have to warn you, if you continue to stare at me, I'm going to be tempted to take things to the next level with a wink. Stare wisely.

Best,
Zehra

Dear White Guy on the Subway,

I want to start by saying I'm sorry about what happened. See, I've been getting a lot of glares lately so I read your look all wrong. It was late in the evening, I was commuting home with a birthday balloon in my hand because I was having a friend visit and wanted to embarrass her with the balloon. I didn't think through that I would be the one that carried it on the subway. Anyway, you kept staring at me. And I just wanted to get home.

I was grateful when my stop came, but then you got up and exited with me. I was a little nervous. Times have changed. You could be a criminal with a gun eager to tell me to get the hell out of this country, inform me about my oppression with a gun to my head. I've got a healthy sense of imagination and fear. So anyway, I started walking a bit faster, up the stairs, and down the street. But you sped up your pace too. And then I was really worried.

But then. With both of us walking at unnaturally fast paces, building up copious amounts of lactic acid in our leg muscles, you caught up and turned to me with a big smile on your face and said, "Assalamu'Alaykum! And Happy Birthday!" before you walked away.

I definitely did not see that coming...

Best,
Zehra

Dear Parents at the Store,

Your toddler isn't bothering me. He's looking at the bright piece of fabric on my head and is mesmerized by it. He's naturally curious. He's not disturbing me, but you trying to turn him away is kinda worrying. I shot a big smile at him and hope he remembers that rather than you pulling him away from me like I'm a leper.

Best,
Zehra (a.k.a. Lady in Changing Room #2)

Dear New Muslim Friend at Work,

You saw the announcement at work about new employees and you saw one of them was a fellow Muslim, a woman wearing a headscarf. Thank you for looking me up, stopping by to say hello during my first week, and checking in on me at least once a week since then. And thank you for saying you were so proud to see a Muslim sister join the ranks of attorneys at the firm. That kind of support is very humbling.

Best,
Zehra

Dear Muslim Auntie #1,

I was just waiting in the buffet line at a wedding, minding my business when you found me, looked more closely at me, and tried to place me. Then suddenly, you recognized me, and this funny look crept over your face – like you thought you saw something weird and you peered closer and confirmed it was worse than you imagined. Like chocolate turning out to be poo. But what you said was, "Oh, you started doing hijab? When did you start *that*? Okay, well good for you". Auntie, I get the feeling you didn't really mean that.

Best,
Zehra

Dear Muslim Auntie #2,

I came by at a wedding to say *salaam* to you. You stopped midway in your conversation and turned to face me, stood to hug me, and then whispered to me during the hug, "I have to say it. I'm so very proud of you. You're the kind of rôle model I want for my daughter. God bless you". Auntie, I get the feeling you really meant that.

Best,
Zehra

Dear Muslim Auntie #3,

It's true, wearing the head covering may put a damper on my chances of getting married. But can we get honest for a minute? Whatever I've done to ward off your son, I've done it successfully for thirty-six years. Let's not deny *me* the credit for driving him off for all these years all on my own. Let's credit the scarf with other things. And Auntie, you get to keep that gem of a son all to yourself. Win-win!

Best,
Zehra

Dear Everyone,

Yes, it's summer, so it is, in fact, getting hot in here, under my scarf. A day later, yep, still hot. And just for sake of thoroughness, talking about how hot I am isn't helping me cool down. I like talking about ice cream, Antarctica, winter, and air conditioning. Let's talk about those. Actually, the entire time you're talking to me, I'm fantasizing about going to Antarctica in the winter, with the air conditioning on full blast, and ice cream in hand. Yeah, that's much better...

Best,
Zehra

Dear Muslim Community,

You just picked at how I'm tying my scarf. You also remarked that my pants could be looser. And that perhaps I shouldn't be going to a certain place or hanging out with certain friends while wearing the scarf.

Lately, many of you have weighed in on my choices: how I define hijab, why I do a particular form of hijab, how I observe hijab. Everyone has their own take on my practice of our shared faith and wants me to know it. Some of you mean well, but you all want me to live up to your interpretation of our shared faith. I didn't sign up for that and it's a battle I couldn't win anyway.

Luckily, I'm not trying to win. Not with you, anyway. In everything I do, I try to keep one thing in mind – does it bring me closer to the best version of myself? Does it help me connect to a greater purpose and serve the greater good? It would be great if we could encourage each other's efforts and support each other on this shared journey. I want us to take the high road and recognize our aims are the same but we may differ slightly on the route.

But if we're not taking the high road, please do let me know, and I'll be happy to write up a list of what I think you can do better too.

Best,

Zehra

Dear Girlfriend,

You're taking a really long time to get ready for this get-together. Did you just snap at me that styling your hair takes a while and I should remember what that's like? I mean, *maybe* I didn't wash my hair today, but I still have to style my scarf just right. There is a world of YouTube tutorials on a bazillion styles of wrapping your headscarf. I mean, I just do the one style really, but don't for a minute think I didn't have options to upgrade my fashion game. What you see here is my refusal to do it. That's a personal choice...but yeah, it's totally better than fussing with the drier/straightener and I don't envy you at this moment. But still, get a move on. I'm hungry.

Best,

Zehra

Dear Muslim Friends,

It's still just me. You get that, right? Some of you knew me back in high school when I first started covering, so this isn't new to you at all, but things coming full circle. But for others of you, I have to admit, it's a bit awkward. Let's write it out.

Apparently, showing up wearing a head covering serves as a trigger for certain conversations. Unsolicited, people like to tell me their views on hijab. People like to tell me about all the times they almost took on the head covering. People like to tell me about why they stopped covering. I mean, okay, that's cool, we can discuss all of that and I'm genuinely interested, but can we actually order the brunch that we came here to eat first?

Also, I just want to be clear, I don't have the power to detect *halal/haram* foods, absolve you of personal choices, or excuse you from certain religious practices. I say that because some of you turn to me at events and ask me if the food is *halal*. I mean, I came with you. Do you think I can somehow sense it, like I have a *halal*-detection superpower? That would be amazing. But I don't. (I'm bummed about that too.)

I also get the feeling you're telling me about why you didn't fast or why you stopped covering because you want me to say it's okay. One, your choices have nothing to do with me and you're assuming I'm awesome at all these practices, which is a huge assumption. Second, I mean, even if I did say it's okay, I'm just speaking for me. I'm not a religious authority just because I'm covering. A piece of fabric does not make it so. I mean I would love to have more power and authority, but I don't. (I'm bummed about that too.)

All this behavior is giving me a weird complex. When I walk into the room, people start checking what they're doing, how they're behaving, what they're wearing. It's a bit odd. If you all keep this up, I will start brushing the end of my scarf to your foreheads and tell you, "By the authority given to me (read: none), I absolve you of your stupidity."

Best,
Zehra

Dear Clothing Designers,

I was always a conservative dresser so I always found shopping difficult. That whole rule about exposing one body part for sexiness – either legs, arms, cleavage, back, or legs? Totally not my bag. The low cut jeans are a nightmare. This sheer ¾ length slip style infuriates me because it's *almost* what I need it to be, but then just as my eyes optimistically skim down the length of the dress, I see where the slip stops short, and I'm thwarted. The sheer thing slays me. Layering is the hijabi girl's friend. I know. But do you know how difficult it is to layer things in the summer? Help a sister out.

Gimme some breezy high neckline, opaque, long sleeve blouses and tunics, some bright print dresses that don't dip into cleavage, some opaque slacks that don't narrow, tighten, squeeze, hoist, or uplift. Gimme that bootcut, flowy, airy goodness. That's what I'm talking about. The modest fashion industry is catching on, but it's still a bit boutiquey out there. I need it to go mainstream enough to give me options where I already shop. Speed up fashionistas…I'm waiting on you.

Best,
Zehra

Dear Scarf Sister in Starbucks during Ramadan,

This year, for the first time in many years, I was not fasting. As you know, there are a lot of reasons why Muslims may not fast during Ramadan, but unless those excuses are visible (age, health, pregnancy), you may get judged by other Muslims. And so there I am, hungry, steps away from a yummy egg and cheese on croissant at the Dunkin Donuts in my building, but I don't want to be judged. So I skip it. Then, during lunch, I passed a woman giving out falafel samples. I almost went for it, but, just at that moment, two women wearing scarves passed by and I lost my nerve. Staying away from the *halal* carts as well, for obvious reasons.

You see, I'm still relatively new at this and it's hitting me that the whole scarf outing me as a Muslim thing can make things a bit awkward to navigate during Ramadan. You know this, I know.

So when I walk into a Starbucks to wait for a friend, and then see you there, I know we both froze, as if we caught each other doing something horrible. We looked at each other sheepishly and then looked away. I think we were both thinking the same thing – not about us being adults, having no right to judge others, or the many reasons why we're both not fasting, but that "if I'm here and you saw me, it means you were here too so who are you going to tell?" Having reached this mutual understanding, we both let out sighs of relief, confidently nodded at each other, and went our way. I like your style, girl.

Best,
Zehra

Dear Jewish Commuting Friend,

I see you every morning on my commute. I can't help but notice that you and I share something really cool. We're both wearing articles of faith. Me with my scarf, you with your *kippa* and *payot*. We're both outed to the world as people of faith. And that garners a lot of negative attention at times, so I feel a certain solidarity with you even though we've never spoken to each other.

The only excuse I've had to catch your eye and smile at you was on a Friday when I had luggage in tow and got onto the elevator with you. I asked you what floor I should press for you. You looked up at me, smiled, and told me the bottom floor. You weren't the least bit phased by my scarf. I can't tell you how much it means in my day to have a smile come at me at first glance rather than a double-take or a glare.

And I found it incredibly relatable to be in the elevator with you when the elevator stopped one floor down and a short old coiffed up white woman was about to step onto the elevator, saw the two of us as she placed one foot in, and then inelegantly yelped and abruptly stepped right out, until her younger companion dragged her back in, glaring at her, and looking at us apologetically.

Best,

Zehra

Dear Ammi,

Thank you for letting me shape my own journey. You worried, you prayed, you humoured me, and you didn't stand in my way. Whatever you did, you have always done to protect me, but it's tough to know the line between protection and interference. Thank you for treading that line so carefully. It's made all the difference, not only in my life, but the lives of all those whose lives I touch.

I am the strangest blend of traditional and modern and, while I'd like to take the credit/blame for that, you share that blessing/burden. Thank you for letting me be strange and test boundaries and explore change. In the end, I've always come right back to the core values you've instilled in me and seen the wisdom in what you said all along. I know you love your "I told you so's" and this pretty much gives you a badge to wave in my face in that regard. You've earned it. I love you and you have always been and remain the greatest blessing in my life.

Best,

Zehra

Dear Muslim Girls and Women Struggling with Whether to Don a Scarf,

A lot of you have reached out to me since I started writing about my decision to wear the headscarf as an adult. You want me to help you figure out if it's going to be good for you or if it's okay to take it off. I can't answer that. I am a big believer in personal journeys. My journey saw me wearing the scarf as a teenager, becoming a de-jabi as a young adult, and then becoming a re-jabi in my adulthood. I wouldn't have taken on the scarf again but for covering and uncovering when I was younger. I needed the full perspective to appreciate the idea of this kind of modesty and to understand which way I preferred, and which brought out the best in me.

I will also tell you that wearing the scarf doesn't feel like a burden or hardship to me. If that's what it feels like to you, then maybe you're doing a disservice to yourself, the idea of hijab, and to those who wear the headscarf. If I had worn it out of a sense of obligation alone, it wouldn't have lasted. I wore it because I knew I wanted to, that I felt fierce with it, and that no matter what came at me because of wearing it, I couldn't imagine not wearing it from that day on.

As you can tell by the series of letters above, there are some incredibly positive experiences that come out of wearing the scarf, and then there are the bad ones. I anticipated the bad ones, and am pleasantly surprised at the many good ones. It's rare that I'll manage to go a full day in New York without a stranger saying *salaam* to me on the streets. That tears me from my self-absorption and self-involvement and forces me to see the other person, acknowledge humanity, community, and brotherhood. I'm richer for that experience. It's what prayer is supposed to be. But because encounters with strangers necessitate interaction with people, you can't tune out the same way some might during prayers. For prayer, you have to step away from your day and commit energy to meditating and reconnecting with your faith. But when someone says *salaam* to you, it is a pleasant invasion into your day. You haven't done anything to warrant it other than go about your day wearing a head covering. It honestly feels like a blessing to me.

But I don't want to sugarcoat it. It will bring down a lot of cusses on you too. You have to be ready to be much more aware of your surroundings. In this world, we can't be oblivious to the prevalence of Islamophobia and people who wish Muslims harm without knowing any of us personally. So you will have to be comfortable giving up your anonymity and your ability to disappear into a crowd. Be prepared for some harassment, many stares and glares, and some downright anxiety and anger-inducing inquiries, critiques, and commentaries.

On the whole, it's been overwhelmingly positive for me. I've had one terrible verbal attack on the train, and yes, I get stared at a lot. But, as a New Yorker I have the street savvy to keep my guard up. That said, on the heels of 9/11, I know too many stories of terrible things that happened to women who wore head covering. So I do understand the safety concerns. I also can't deny that it may hamper your career trajectory depending on your colleagues, workplace, and field. Can a female wearing a head covering be a litigator or a TV reporter? Yes, but she will have more of an uphill battle. That's not to discourage her; it actually means there's a pressing need for her.

Jut never let it become something you resent. Figure out your own choices and journey, know the pros and cons and know what you can handle. I can't tell you what is best for you. I can only tell you my experiences and my thoughts on my journey so far. To me, it hasn't just been worth it, it's been rewarding beyond my imagination.

Best,
Zehra

PART 2

THE DISTRIBUTION OF NORMAL

Veiled to Speak: Finding a Voice in Doha's *Souq*
E. Dawson Varughese

> *"Living in this world is like walking on a sand dune.*
> *It's impossible not to change the world as one walks."*
> ~Anil Menon, *Half of What I Say*

Doha's Iranian market doesn't look like it used to. These days, *souq waqif* resembles something like a film set, celebrating the heritage of an erstwhile *khaleeji* town; beautifully smooth, cream-washed walls, luxurious woodwork and a perfectly paved walkway underfoot. It is something of a surreal experience to walk around the Iranian *souq* nowadays when you have known it in its previous incarnations. Yet it remains a place of trade, commerce and cultural exchange, busy and enjoyable.

In the early 2000s I was living and working in Doha, teaching by day and shopping by evening. At the beginning, most of my purchases were out of necessity, but a few months in the shopping became more about discovery than need. As such, the Iranian *souq* was there to be discovered.

I was always "covered" in Qatar. It was an easy transition for me as my fashion had usually been of long and voluminous tastes and, with my interests in South Asia, covering my head with a *dupatta* was second-nature. So when I say that I "covered" in Qatar what I mean to say is that I covered like a South Asian.

"*Anti min wain? Anti min Pakistan, min Kashmir?* Where are you from? Are you from Pakistan, from Kashmir?" These were the words of shopkeepers, tailors, taxi drivers.

Sure enough, the colours, the styles, the "look" was clearly not that of *a khaleeji*, or Gulf Arab, but I was covered even if I wasn't veiled as such. This regular questioning never really bothered me and, after some months living in Qatar, I would embellish my identity narratives – just a tiny bit – to keep them interesting and alive. I could be Kashmiri, *Lebnani* or *Irani*, all credible identities that were both given and proffered throughout the days in Doha.

This strategy of identity formation wasn't an outright lie, my aim was not to create some imaginary fantastical self — because, you see, I've never really

97

searched for the "one self". I realize that, for others, such a statement may be alarming and disconcerting. To be several selves – and demonstrably so – can (mis)communicate to others that you are fickle or untrustworthy, a shape-shifter of sorts. The monolithic self, unchanging and steadfast, is certainly a precept of Western identity-formation in my experience, especially when juxtaposed to, say, non-European notions in which fate — *maktoob, naseeb,* or *kismet* — shape and frame you and your time on earth (and beyond). To be ever-changing, therefore, is a natural state in my opinion, even at the level of the quotidian. Harnessing this position allowed me to comfortably "be" according to the situation.

And being chameleon in my identity suited me. It gave me an eye and ear into other worlds. It was my conviction in the benefits of a multi-faceted self that gave me the confidence to visit the Iranian *souq,* not simply covered, but veiled.

By this point, I had bought two *abayas.* One was an edge-to-edge *abaya* with beautiful designs tracing the long hemline, sides and edges, the other was a "full" *abaya,* complete with hijab and *niqab.* I had taken some time choosing this one. It had to be right. It wasn't simply a coat or an outer garment — it was an outfit. What you choose to have (or not) on your *abaya* in terms of colour, stitching and embellishments matters. It does, after all, say something about you — the "you" that is inside – for when you are veiled, it is the veil that communicates a sense of personal identity, an identity that is not visible to the outside world. My *abaya* was a medium weight one with maroon and deep green embroidery in the style of small flowers and vines. There were no diamantes or rhinestones adorning its edges or the corners of my hijab — a fashion that was very much in vogue at the time.

Veiling, when you have not been brought up to do so, takes time. The trickiest element for me was tying the hijab tight enough around my head to keep my hair in place and then the placing of the *niqab* to sit comfortably and correctly over my nose and mouth, letting only my eyes peek through. I remember how the *niqab* fell softly on my face. The warm breeze from the Corniche made it flutter around my cheeks and lips. I could see out, but no one could see in. My world – me – became all the more immediate when I was veiled. I felt myself encroach upon "me" and this was, at times, uncomfortable as I didn't want that kind of proximity to myself, to my worries, concerns and imperfections. Other times, it was comforting, my world within the folds and sways of the black gown, accessible only to me — most importantly for the Iranian *souq*, a "me" that was not revealed to anyone with whom I would interact. There were no limits to whom I could be, providing that I was careful to get the things that people would "see" of me right.

The most obvious aspect of me to be revealed in the Iranian *souq* was my language. This was going to be my identity marker. Those with whom I interacted would form their idea of my identity from the language I spoke and, moreover, the fluency and the accent with which I spoke it. I had been learning Arabic before my arrival in Qatar but practising the language had proven difficult without a barrage of "identity questions". I figured that the veil would give me the chance finally to speak, to find my voice, and therein my social experiment was conceived.

Standing a short distance from the Iranian *souq* I knew what I wanted to buy, only a few incidental items: *qawa* (coffee), *bukhoor* (incense), a kitchen item or two, and a hair clip. As I approached the Iranian *souq* I realized that I was not at all noticeable. In fact, I believed that I was almost invisible. I relaxed. From behind the veil, the place looked different. Although I could see out quite comfortably from behind my *niqab*, I couldn't see everything as I normally did. I had lost a kind of panorama. This closing in of landscape and perspective was both isolating and liberating. I felt alone because, in veiling, I had brought myself in. I panicked as I realized that I lacked my usual warmth and expression. But the space that was created by the veil, the geography between me and the Iranian *souq*, was also liberating and I felt a certain confidence in stepping into the world of the various, male merchants.

The veil made me focus, and yet, it gave me time to look around, to browse comfortably. It dispelled any invitations to look at this and that. No one bothered to invite me to look at the various wares, and I felt a sense of freedom in those moments. This experience, the silence in which I moved around the *souq*, was part of finding a voice. I was there, I was present – *ana mowjooda* — and I was everything I needed to be to engage in commerce. I had a voice. I wasn't however, going to purchase my shopping in silence, and so when I found my first items – *qawa* and *bukhoor* – I was going to have to speak.

When I speak French, most Francophones know that I have lived in Paris and when I speak Hindi, I rely on Urdu over Sanskrit words because I make the

99

connection with the Arabic I still have shelved away somewhere in my head. I knew in the Iranian *souq* that, from behind the veil, my accent and my choice of Arabic words would speak volumes. It wasn't simply a question of finding the Arabic for what I wanted to say, it was a question of finding the *khaleeji* Arabic for what I wanted to say. Only a few sounds could give me away and destroy the façade that I had so carefully crafted in my clothing.

My mind wandered back to the further education classes which were housed in a depressed corner of an English city, the Egyptian teacher welcoming me to learn Arabic. All the other girls at the institute were Pakistani. They were learning the Qur'an and *tajweed* – recitation pronunciation – was one of the first Arabic words I learned. My teacher held up a mirror to my face and asked me to repeat after her: "ah" for "ahmed", "qa" for "Qatar", "ayn" for "ali".

"Look into the mirror, feel your throat, see what you are doing to make these sounds. Don't worry, *inshaAllah,* they will come. *InshaAllah*, one day, you will say them."

She was right. The sounds did eventually come and, when I moved to Qatar, I realized that my "ah", my "qa" and my "ayn" all needed more gusto than I had previously given them. I remembered my teacher fondly on many occasions and I often wondered what had become of her.

These were the thoughts and images in my mind as I stood in the Iranian *souq* all those years after the "mirror" lesson. I bought my *qawa* with pronunciational ease – both my teacher and the veil made this possible. Although an exchange of everyday greetings, the request for an item and its payment is basic in terms of language proficiency. Being veiled gave me the confidence in those early days to speak and to find my own voice in Doha's Iranian *souq*.

Other visits to the Iranian *souq* allowed me to test my Arabic further and, in time, I developed both pronunciation and vocabulary, returning home to write it all up in my notebook. I'm sure to this day that the traders in the Iranian *souq* wondered at my accent, at my identity, but unlike other instances out and about in Doha where I was only "covered", I never came to know the questions that the vendors held on their lips. I suspect they thought I was Iranian or Pakistani but this guess is probably because these were the identities I was "given" when I was unveiled. I didn't wear gloves in the *souq* and, from this alone, I suspect some of the vendors made their educated guesses, not least because of the stones I wore set in rings of yellow Indian gold. At times, I was served by Baluchis, Pakistanis or Afghanis, and there was often a moment of hesitation as I wondered if I would be addressed in Baluchi, Urdu or Pashto, but of course that never happened. I was veiled, after all. And so this agreed silence, by virtue of the veil, allowed me to develop and grow in Qatar in ways that I would have otherwise never known.

Hijab, Niqab, Thongs, and Pac Man
Louise Lambert

> *"Through others we become ourselves."*
> ~Lev S. Vygotsky

I am not Muslim. Let's just start there. I am a white, Christian Canadian, entirely raised in the Western world. Now, I am a professor in the United Arab Emirates with students who are primarily Muslim. As a result, I've seen fashionable young women parade through the halls in every style of hijab. From the *shayla* – a thin cloth that can be beautifully worn tight across the entire head, light and slipping off the forehead, barely hanging off the hair bun at the back, or wrapped up tight and swept up high African style – to the more severe-looking *niqab*, where women mask their faces behind a black curtain.

I have no problem with the *shayla*. *Shayla* head coverings are a fashion statement worth appreciating. The *shayla* wearer takes great pride in tying, tucking, getting the angle just right, matching, inserting, and pinning. When it is done, the effect is slick and trendy – a far cry from my unruly hair, which often has no style at all. *Shaylas* can match shoes, pants, tops, and even eye shadow. Ultimately, they match unique personalities.

I like these students that come to my class in their fashion-forward headscarves. I can connect with them. When they smile, I find myself smiling. Their eyes crinkle and so do mine in return. The hijab is a piece of clothing, adornment. It doesn't interfere with my relationship to these women.

But when it comes to the *niqab*, I have a complicated relationship.

Sitting here in the UAE today, I'll be honest, I don't like it. I don't feel a warm and empathetic bond with a woman wearing *niqab* in the same way I do with a woman without. I can't see her eyes, face, smile, dimples, or smirk. I can't tell if she is rolling her eyes at me or grimacing in ridicule or disagreement. I even try extra hard to smile, to look at the space where her eyes should be and express without words, "Hey! I like you! I am trying to connect with you!"

But, it is a one-sided conversation. I can't mimic her emotions because I can't see them. I can't truly connect with her. It's like talking to a computer – she talks back but it is hollow, devoid of any real feeling. So I try harder. I search for the emotion in her voice, that tell-tale spark that will give her covered form a distinct persona. But I must not be good at it. Or maybe the voice just doesn't carry the range of emotion the face does.

I feel lonely, shut out, dismissed. Our relationship – if one can even call it that – is a purely functional one. That's not to say that they are invisible. I have talkative students that don the *niqab*. Their comments in class are smart, funny, and insightful. I really want to know them more on a personal level, but because I work at a coeducational university, they keep their *niqab*s over their faces so the men can't see them. I'd like to be able to stop them in the hallway and say hello. But, I can't tell them apart from other *niqab*-covered students. I want to share a smile with them, but they are masked and I am at a disadvantage. They can like me, know me, see me, but I don't get the same privilege. And yet, I am a woman too. Am I so awful that you need protection from me? Or might you just be so fabulous that you need protection from yourself? I guess I don't really understand why – I just know that it's alienating and it pushes me away.

It's shocking how much body language contributes to human connection. There was a time, only a few years ago when I was the *niqabi*. And the bliss I felt then is at odds with the negative feelings the *niqab* evokes in me now.

As I said, my relationship with *niqab* is complicated.

In 2004, I went to study Arabic in Yemen. To be clear, I had no intention of donning black as I planned my journey. My goal was to learn the language and observe the culture by interacting with locals. Upon arriving, however, it became obvious that I stood out. And not in a pleasant way. Being a Westerner and taller than many of those around me was just part of the problem. My clothing also set me apart. For one thing, I was wearing colour – a stark contrast to the black robes all the women wore in public. And while I thought my pants and top were loose and modest, as I walked down the streets, it became clear that I was on everyone's radar. Eyes boring into the back of my head were bad enough, but feeling eyes on me as I was walked towards people brought a whole other sense of vulnerability. I felt different, self-conscious. Despite having clothes on, I felt as if I was out in public wearing nothing more than a bikini. No one said anything or acted disrespectfully; in fact, they were really trying hard to ignore my near nakedness. But I was the one intruding on their social order. I felt it viscerally. The discomfort was palpable, almost like when you blurt out something totally stupid and your face gets red hot and your ears ring. You feel like an ant, but no one says a word. Somehow, that feels even worse.

I decided to blend in as much as possible. I decided I would wear the *abaya*, hijab, and *niqab* over the coming weeks. It was fun, almost like playing dress-up every morning. I took to *abaya*-shopping with enthusiasm. I was enveloped in a world of store keepers bringing out cups of welcome tea, a world of hand gestures where strangers would take my measure.

"Too long, she needs longer," they would say. "Western girls are very tall."

Nervous laughter would ensue and little boys spying at the door of the open shop would giggle. I was so clueless and felt almost childlike as ladies tried to show me how to wrap a proper hijab. I was an amateur, so I needed plenty of pins to hold the fabric in place. But it was the *niqab* that turned out to be the crowning piece. I didn't really need this piece, to be honest. Covering the body and hair was enough. But I thought, when in Rome... And it would be fun, I argued with myself. It'll make a good story back home. So I put on the *niqab* and headed out to the street.

And, I won't lie, it was bliss.

So much for Westernized notions of fashion and dress. I was enjoying the perks of being a *niqabi* in an Arab society. It was a massive sea change from my experience thus far as a foreigner. No one stared, no one threw rocks. People moved out of my way, people opened doors for me, men carried things for me. I walked into a restaurant and was immediately seated away from teenage boys and single men. My anonymity demanded respect and privilege. I had been elevated from the ranks of "cheap naked Westerner" to self-respecting woman. I could see everyone and no one could see the real me. I was incognito, communicating without having to use words. I was suddenly afforded a ton of respect, no longer an outsider.

And, most importantly, I didn't have to be self-conscious of my own body. Others could not gaze upon it. My self-esteem climbed as I realized that I didn't have to obsess over my flaws and imperfections. Clothes became secondary. I could wear shorts and a t-shirt under my *abaya*, and I was nowhere near as hot as I had been previously under the Yemeni sun. The thin black gauzy material lifted the heat away. Fretting over my hair became a thing of the past. There was no need to think of clothes or appearance. We were all uniform and there was a freedom in that.

It wasn't until I returned to the UAE that I noticed the difference. Suddenly, I was on show again, standing at certain angles so my stomach looked thinner.

I found myself opting to wear one pair of jeans instead of another because one made my thighs look fatter. The difference was stark and my mood changed accordingly. But, more than anything, I felt how I had changed. Wearing an *abaya* had elevated me. Suddenly, I demanded a lot more respect from the world around me. As a *niqabi*, I had felt more powerful if only because I could observe others and yet remain anonymous myself.

But the shoe is on the other foot now and I realize that I don't like the *niqab* one bit. I am the one being observed and it makes me uncomfortable. It makes me feel unsafe. Recently, a high-profile murder happened in Abu Dhabi. A *niqabi* woman stabbed a Western woman at an upscale shopping mall on Reem Island. Security footage clearly showed the attacker, covered head to foot, stalking her prey. Since then I have hated the *niqab* even more. The anonymity that I enjoyed while in Yemen is unfair to the rest of the world. The *niqabi* in her black curtain can see us but we can't see her. We don't know if there is a weapon or even if the *niqab* is hiding a man under its folds. Is she smiling, scowling, angry, insulted or insulting us? Somehow the inequity of it didn't really occur to me when I was the one walking with pride, confident in my power that no one else could see me unless I allowed it. I was enveloped in mystery oblivious to the barrier that it created with those around me.

Our face is the first and most powerful way we connect with one another as people. It's how we decide whether to trust someone or not. It's how we decide whether they are lying or genuine, whether they think we are clever and funny or if they are bored by our presence. In *niqab*, there no way to make a connection. It may seem hypocritical for me to say this, especially as I had once taken advantage of the same anonymity. But, at the time, it was an experiment in change. A chance to try something different — be someone different — for a little bit.

In hindsight, I think my own brief period in *niqab* was a missed opportunity for me. Had I opted not to wear a *niqab* in Yemen, I'm fairly confident that I would have eventually become accustomed to the stares and could have overcome the cultural barriers through my smile and the hilarity of my Arabic mispronunciations. It would have been a human connection based on my individuality. Being covered, however, robbed me of the chance truly to connect on any meaningful level. And I think the loss was mutual. The Yemenis I interacted with missed the chance to get to know a Western woman who is genuinely interested in their culture. I lost the ability really to learn about their ways, stories and relationships by hiding behind a thin piece of gauze in my quest to be a real "lady." I won't say that it wasn't a fun experiment for me as an individual, but I think the barrier it created resulted in a greater loss of potential understanding between two worlds.

No, I don't like *niqab*. But I will defend a woman's right to wear it.

My time in the Muslim world has changed me fundamentally. I go home to North America and am shocked at how little clothes people have on. True, the environment shapes our attitudes and views and I have become more conservative as a result of being here. Yet, I am shocked at how shocked I am. Have "we" always walked around with so few garments? Did I used to walk around this way? Apparently yes, but I never thought of myself as inappropriately dressed before and now everywhere I look there are butt cracks, flabby arms, wrinkled and not-so-wrinkled cleavages, elephant knees, muffin tops, arm pit hairs, back hairs... I could go on. Oh please, someone put some clothes on all of these bodies!

It's not that the *niqab* would be of any help with the thong line. But maybe, just maybe, the *niqab* might instill some appropriateness, some modesty, some respectability, some cover so that we all don't need to see so much skin on the street that we feel uncomfortable. It makes my mood drop. Everyone seems classless, baseless, crass; lacking in self-respect. I don't want a relationship with these people, yet, they are my people, aren't they? It's a confusing dialogue to have in my own head.

Nowadays, I find it even harder to tolerate Westerners who can't stop criticizing the hijab and *niqab* while visiting me in Dubai.

"Do they really wear those drowning machines at the beach? They look like Pac Man," one visiting friend said to me as she took in the sight for the first time.

"Seriously, why do you defend a woman's right to disrobe but not to cover up?" I shot back. "Aren't we supposed to defend freedom in the West? Doesn't freedom mean being able to do as you please or is freedom only good when it fits with 'our' notion of 'normal'?" I tried not to get angry but her criticisms were getting to me.

"Are you converting to Islam or something?"

Sigh.

I was pretty pissed but to be honest, I was in a bit of a jam myself. I don't like *niqab* for my personal reasons, but I wouldn't stop anyone from covering up. On the other hand, I will defend *niqab* just to prove a point that freedom should mean freedom for all, and not just freedom for you to be like me. That type of grey thinking is not always easy to explain in a black-and-white world.

Like I said, my relationship with *niqab* is complicated.

#Islamophobia: A Non-Muslim Faces the Prejudice
Caitlin Elaine

"We can never judge the lives of others, because each person knows only their own pain and renunciation. It's one thing to feel that you are on the right path, but it's another to think that yours is the only path."
~Paulo Coelho

I do not wear the hijab. I am not Muslim. In fact, in spite of being raised in the heart of the Bible Belt in the southern United States, I am not very religious at all. I do believe, more than anything, in respecting and learning from other people and seeing things from new perspectives.

My focus during my undergraduate degree was in archaeology, but my degree course was an all-inclusive programme through which I was able to do research in both archaeology and cultural anthropology. By my final semester I had traveled to India twice and spent three months working in Oman, all for course credit. My experiences in Oman inspired not only a career shift towards the Arab world and away from South Asia, but a keen interest in Islam and the role of women in the religion. I wanted to know more than what the right-wing Western media tells us.

Upon my return from Oman, I was asked to be part of a campus planning committee to develop a program that would celebrate a region of the world for one academic year. I was in a particularly advantageous position because the region selected for the upcoming year was the Arabian Peninsula. Needless to say, I was eager to contribute! Anything to take me back to the Middle East, even metaphorically, made me happy.

Among the events proposed was one during which non-Muslim women who typically adhered to American clothing styles would wear the hijab for a day. The aim of this activity was to show support for Muslim women who choose to wear the hijab and to see what it was like to be veiled. As I needed a subject for my senior capstone, I thought to accomplish two things at once by volunteering to develop the hijab idea into a combined university event and research project.

In the initial development stages, I delved into the academic literature on the hijab. I read a study in which interpersonal discrimination was measured for varying forms of veiling including no veil at all. The study by King and

Ahmad (2010) found that interpersonal discrimination was greater for the hijab and the full veil. Another study noted that women who wore the hijab in Western countries had a more positive body image than those who did not because they felt less pressure to adhere to unrealistic beauty standards (Swami *et.al*, 2013). One study even found that hijabi women tended to have a healthier emotional state despite increased discrimination. This was likely because they felt more secure in their decision to satisfy what they considered to be a religious commandment (Jasperse *et.al*, 2012).

I also spoke with women in the Muslim Student Association (MSA) at my university and women from a local Islamic educational group and found that each of them felt differently about their hijabs. The core reasoning was all the same – to please Allah – but the ways in which they practised this were widely varied. From "hijabi-fashionista" styles to minimalistic hijabs, each had her own way of doing what they collectively believed was right. One woman mentioned that she had not chosen to wear the hijab until she was an adult. She told me that it allowed her to stop worrying about what she looked like and what other people thought of her appearance. She felt that it enabled her to focus more on developing what was inside — her intelligence and her heart — and allowed people to focus more on what she said rather than what she looked like.

I began planning my research and determined that, to be sufficiently thorough, I would have two parts to the project. Working with the MSA and local leaders in the Islamic community, I developed a survey for the general public. This survey requested demographic information from participants and asked them to rank several stereotypes about the hijab on a Likert scale from one (agree) to five (disagree). Anyone could complete this survey and I planned to use it as a baseline for the general opinion on campus. The second part was a bit more complex, and required volunteers to take the general survey, to wear the hijab for a day or more, and then participate in a second survey and/or focus group. I had organized two campus-wide events during which I would recruit volunteers for the research. At each of these events, I scheduled speakers to teach about the hijab from a scholarly perspective and discuss their personal experiences and decisions to wear the hijab.

All of this was planned out to the letter, including the obligatory disclaimers about participation being entirely voluntary and letting participants know that they could remove the hijab at any point for any reason, especially if they felt unsafe. Prior to submitting the project for approval, I had a preliminary meeting with the chair of the research board. In this meeting, I was assured that this was a simple project and that I should be able to get quick approval without a formal board meeting to discuss it. As I was under the impression that everything would progress smoothly, I submitted the project for approval. I should have known that nothing is ever that easy.

A day or two after I submitted the research proposal, a local conservative online media outlet published a scathing Letter to the Editor which had been written as a response to the university's press release about the Arabian Peninsula Program. The author of the letter accused the university of having a "radical" pro-Islamic agenda. Readers, of course, chimed in on the comment board. One commenter even threatened to bring images of beheaded children to the hijab events! Thankfully, there were some who challenged the author of the letter and countered the voices of those who agreed with the author's narrow-minded perspective.

However, as soon as this letter and the associated comments hit the email circuit at the university, I received several emails and calls from professors and people who had helped me organize these events. Next thing I knew, we had enlisted extra security for the events, and within a day I had an email saying that my research would require a full review by the board and that the board would not meet again for another month. With the hijab events only two weeks away, I realized that things were not going to be as simple as I had hoped. I was encouraged to submit a second application with just the general survey so that I would be able to get started on the project. I did this, received approval, and was met within the same week with an informal request to hold off until I had spoken with some other people to make sure the survey was the best it could be in order to get the best data. It was at this point that I realized that the stars might have been aligning against me and time was running out. The longer I put off doing the research, the less time I had to work with the data and create a final product for my capstone.

After all the research I had done with literature and interviews, I knew I needed to wear the hijab to experience it myself, if only for a few days. I had worn a scarf a few times in India and Oman but the experience is vastly different when covering the head is the societal norm. I wanted to know what it was like to be a hijabi for a few days in America.

During the two days on which we held the events, I wore the hijab full time. I dressed modestly and had regularly to check my scarf to make sure it had not fallen off. On the whole, the experience was not so different from my hijab-less days. If anything, I felt more confident because my appearance seemed less important. My clothes were loose and my head was covered. I felt like I wasn't being constantly judged for the shape of my body.

Photo courtesy of Caitlin Elaine

The campus events were surprisingly successful. No one showed up with horrific signs in protest and I had a great time learning and helping to educate others about the hijab. However, because my research was still pending approval, I wasn't allowed to discuss it publicly. So, when a reporter from the same conservative online media outlet showed up and interviewed me, I was limited in what I could tell him. Because I couldn't discuss the project publicly until it was approved, I was unable to tell him that the events were supposed to be part of my capstone research. I could not even specify what the research was about. I didn't think it would be a significant issue. I rather naïvely hoped that perhaps I had opened an avenue of education by speaking to the media.

Within the next day or so, it became obvious that the reporter had no intention of promoting the positive message of the events and managed, albeit rather tactfully on his part, to misrepresent me and my goals. While he got most of the information correct about the events and even accurately quoted me in parts, he used his own phrasing to spin the viewpoint that I was wearing the hijab to "see if I got any mean looks." Those words stared back at me, taunting and belittling my efforts to understand the hijab from within. I wanted to scream at the reporter, "You don't know my intentions! This was my research! How can I research the hijab if I haven't experienced it?"

By putting a negative spin on my use of the hijab during the events, the reporter basically invalidated the quotation that followed in which I talked about breaking stereotypes and understanding how prevalent misconceptions about the hijab are. This was the first time since taking on the project that I felt truly discouraged. Despite all the hurdles I had faced, I had managed to stay positive about the project up to that point. But seeing my own words contorted and used against me was entirely inconceivable and heartbreaking.

Within the same week I was contacted by a representative at a local public radio station, who requested an interview. Public radio is generally less biased than other media outlets and it seemed that they were genuinely interested in the project, but naturally I was hesitant, uncertain of their motives. I finally decided that it was important to take the chance. The interview went smoothly and was broadcast as part of a larger national radio show. It was almost as if someone knew that I needed a little encouragement to keep the research project going.

In the time after the hijab events leading up to the review board meeting, I met with the people that were recommended to me in order to ensure that the survey was acceptable. I made a few small changes, and continued reading the published literature on the hijab. I felt confident that my research would be approved. I genuinely thought that my project was not a risky one and that the review board would agree. But at the meeting we discussed the project as a whole and my research plan was rejected. The board felt that I had not provided enough evidence that I was not putting the volunteers at risk. In spite of a fully-planned briefing session and the fact that the project had been developed in conjunction with people who regularly wear the hijab, I had not presented my case well enough! They encouraged me to resubmit my proposal with better evidence. Unfortunately, my time had run out. I couldn't wait any longer to begin my capstone research. Waiting for the next board meeting would have set me on a timeline to complete my research after my expected graduation date and long after my capstone was due. My only option was to make the best of the general survey which had been approved earlier.

I submitted my project and graduated on time, but I felt as though I had been let down and that I had let others down. It felt incomplete, but there wasn't much more that could be done. I was preparing for my second trip to Oman and I was no longer formally affiliated with the university.

Just as I was settling in to my new life in Oman, something happened that shook the ground beneath me. I stumbled upon something I should have expected, but for which I was not prepared. I came across a website that quoted me from the article about the Arabian Peninsula Project – the same article that had twisted my words and put a damper on the events I had so enthusiastically and diligently worked on. A link to the full article, which contained a photo of me as well as my full name, was also included. Following the excerpt of the article was a stream of vitriolic comments.

Telling myself I should stop, I continued to read every last one of the hundred or so comments, many of which specifically referred to me by name. Terrible insults were thrown at me. One commenter even begged me not to vote. I was called brain-dead, brain-washed, stupid, and indoctrinated. They described Islam as a "deadly mental virus" and accused me of just playing "dress-up". Multiple commenters alluded to me needing to be beaten by a Muslim man so that I could "get some sense knocked into me". Some went out of their way to find my personal information. My LinkedIn account — which I use for professional networking — stated that I was focusing on archaeology and had regional interests in the Arabian Peninsula and South Asia. One commenter took the interpretational liberty to say that, based on my LinkedIn profile, my next step was to join the Islamic State (ISIS). The reporter's phrasing about "mean looks" provided ample ammunition for these commenters. This project was nearly six months in the making, from inception to completion. Yet it suddenly felt like all of my efforts had been a waste. How could I possibly make a difference when all it took was one person – one article — to make people hate me? The comments plagued my mind. I tried to understand what would make someone hate *me* — a complete stranger —

enough to say such dreadful things. It took me some time, but I finally realized. This is precisely what bigotry *is*.

I had wronged them in no way, and yet was treated with unfounded hatred. The Islamophobia was so strong that simply because I wanted to discuss hijab – to educate people about the hijab as a non-Muslim who doesn't even wear the hijab – I put myself on the receiving end of Islamophobic contempt.

I sometimes wonder whether this is a fight I should have been involved in. Because I am not Muslim, I have no stake in this battle, other than the fact that I fully support the women I know who choose to wear the hijab. I feel that forcing women *not* to wear the hijab is the same as forcing women to wear the hijab. In both cases, individual choice is eliminated.

I guess, despite the hurdles – or perhaps because of them — my experiences have taught me that education is a worthy goal. The hatred that I experienced is precisely the thing I hope to help eliminate through education. The vitriol hurt me. I won't deny that. I can empathize with the women who choose to wear hijab and face that hurt on a regular basis. All in all, my resolve to continue learning about the hijab and educating others has been strengthened by experiencing Islamophobia. In true American spirit, my passion for a woman's right to choose has not dampened by the haters. It has intensified.

References

Jasperse, M., Ward, C., & Jose, P. E. (2012). Identity, perceived religious discrimination, and psychological well-being in Muslim immigrant women. *Applied Psychology*, *61*(2), 250-271.

King, E. B., & Ahmad, A. S. (2010). An experimental field study of interpersonal discrimination toward Muslim job applicants. *Personnel Psychology, 63*(4), 881-906.

Swami, V., Miah, J., Noorani, N. & Taylor, D. (2014). Is the hijab protective? An investigation of body image and related constructs among British Muslim women. *British Journal of Psychology, 105*(3), 352-363.

It's Complicated
Patreshia Tkach

"There's so much grey to every story — nothing is so black and white."
~ Lisa Ling

It's complicated, this whole issue about the hijab, the headscarf, covering. The longer I live in the Middle East the more I understand it, and the less I care for it. And even that I find difficult to say because it seems so culturally, religiously insensitive, or naïve. At its best it looks effortless, with style and cultural preference, and religious freedom. At its worst it looks oppressive, imposed, and harshly mandatory.

In the summer of 1994, while hitchhiking in the west of France, I first encountered the controversy of the hijab in the Western world. I had only been in the car for five minutes before the driver went off on it, launching into a politically charged rant about "those people." Those people who were not assimilating like immigrants are supposed to. Those women, *covered like that.* That wasn't French. I had no idea what he was talking about. A few days later I got his point when I passed through a small city and saw two women covered in black from head to toe with metal plates over their eyes and mouth. It was bizarre, I admit.

In 2007 I returned to France. By now the riots in the predominantly Muslim suburbs of Paris were well known, and of course 9/11 had happened, and all eyes turned to the world of Islam with a mixture of questions, critiques, and attempts to understand more. The conversation about what it means to be French was now common, and a judge had recently refused to grant citizenship to an immigrant woman because she showed up in court fully covered, which he said proved she had not assimilated into the French culture — a prerequisite for citizenship.

In 2008 I began teaching at a university in Turkey, a country that at the time was the model of secular Islam. Students mingled easily in the co-ed classrooms and it took me a while to sort out the girls who pulled on a scarf as they left the school building from those who did not. Head scarves were forbidden in public buildings in an effort to separate religion and politics, and had become a rallying cry for religious freedom of expression throughout the country.

Little was said to me initially concerning this controversy about the head scarf, and because I was not able to read Turkish newspapers, I was unaware of how big an issue it truly was, and how complicated the politics of it all were. My female students — both covered and uncovered — strolled arm in arm on campus, and it was not uncommon to see girls who wore the scarf walking in public with boys. From my perspective, the scarf was a minor religious gesture and women seemed content to put their scarf on and take it off as needed. It seemed to me a much tolerated situation. Of course I lived in the western, more liberal part of Turkey, and still, it was not as tolerated as I thought.

In the university classroom there were several styles of dress amongst the young women. Those who wore the scarf outside of class fell into three categories. There were the very conservative girls who wore layers of dull-colored, long skirts and tops that were then covered with a long overcoat buttoned to the neck and belted. To me, these looked oppressively hot, and heavy! There were others who also dressed in long skirts and tops but with colour, and no overcoat. And finally, there were those who wore make up and dressed in a modern style of leggings and jeans and, aside from the scarf, were indistinguishable from most of the other uncovered girls. The very conservatively dressed young women wore thick plain scarves, but the majority had their heads adorned with shiny, bright, colourful scarves which seemed to me to have the opposite of the intended purpose of tamping down their attractiveness. I mentioned this to one of my students when she pulled on her scarf as we left the school building and she just laughed at the paradox.

Likewise in the classroom, progressive ideas about education and the roles of women and men were supported equally from both groups of young women (covered and uncovered). It was far more common for boys in the class to express conservative social opinions, though all of these young men dressed in the western collegiate style of t-shirt and jeans and sported cool, trendy haircuts.

Although I didn't learn a great deal about the Muslim faith while I was in Turkey, I did learn that secular Turks, who looked to the West for their identity and future, were feeling like a minority and were fearful of the political direction in which the country was moving. But in this western part of the country, men and women mingled easily, alcohol was openly sold in the grocery store and restaurants, and there was a new modern shopping mall in town, so I was at first less aware of this pull. When I travelled in the central and eastern parts of the country, where grocery stores did not sell wine and spirits, where towns and villages were dominated by men who walked on the streets and sat around the tea houses, and being an uncovered woman on the street brought non-stop stares, I saw the Turkey they feared being pulled back into. In these parts, the few women I did see (aside from those on college campuses) resembled the most conservative women in my classroom. It looked dull and oppressive, primarily for women. And when I saw women trudging along in the heat of the Anatolian summers in heavy garments, concealing themselves from the eyes of men in deference to their fathers, brothers, husbands, and God, while the men wore knee length shorts, sandals and short sleeved shirts, with the breeze blowing through the hair on their bare heads, it reinforced the image of an archaic world of inequality.

During this same time I had an opportunity to travel to Egypt, where I observed a very similar situation. Although there were some women who dressed in Western styles to some extent, the majority of women of all ages were covered and dressed as in eastern Turkey. I have extended family (through marriage) in Cairo and the young women in the family were mostly of the latter group, though my brother-in-law says it was the opposite when he was growing up. During that era, covered women were the exception, not the norm. I met two cousins there, two sisters, both in college. One was covered and one was not. The older sister, who wore the scarf, was very outspoken about politics and the role of women in Egypt, and she seemed an unlikely candidate to choose to cover when clearly her family did not insist on it. One day in conversation I rather boldly suggested that women covered because of men more than religious zeal. A male cousin was also there at the time and said this was absolutely not true, that women wanted to cover out of modesty and religious morality. The cousin wearing the scarf turned to him and quite emphatically said no, it was because of men. She said it was uncomfortable for a woman to walk down the streets of Cairo uncovered. But she then told me her own decision to cover followed an event in which she believed God had answered a prayer, and in thanks she started wearing the scarf.

During my last semester teaching at the university in Turkey, one of my brightest and most charming students won a Fulbright scholarship to attend a six-week programme in the United States. She came to me one day full of anxiety because a professor had taken her aside and told her she was not to wear a headscarf in America as she was going as a representative of a Turkish university. Turkey was a secular country and the United States was a secular country and it would be inappropriate. Was it true, she asked me, that she should not, could not, wear her scarf there? I proudly told her that in the USA she could decide for herself whether or not to wear the scarf. I had inadvertently landed firmly on the side of those in Turkey who believed that women should be free to cover their heads anywhere at any time, even though by that point I strongly objected to the inequality of the head scarf. It annoyed me that women were expected to defer to men and cover out of modesty, yet men did not similarly cover. And the simple response I received to this inequality when I asked about it was that it was not traditional for men to cover.

It was, however, a comment by a young woman who did not wear the scarf and who seemed the epitome of modern, secular Turkey that upset me the most. She said she would probably start wearing a scarf after she was married out of respect for her husband. Another woman whom I met shortly after her marriage went from wearing short skirts and dyed blond hair to longer dresses and a covered head in the two years I knew her. "It was just less stressful," she said, referring to pressure from her husband and his family. The idea that these young women, brought up in families that did not require them to wear the scarf, would choose to withdraw a part of themselves from the world seemed all wrong.

Having grown up in the male dominated Catholic religion, I am loathe to tolerate any religion that perpetuates the myth of Adam being led astray by Eve. Up until 30 years, Catholicism also required women to cover their heads, with the veil serving as as a symbol of modesty and submission to men, who are seen as the "image and glory of God", according to Corinthians 11:3 to 16 in the Bible. The Catholic Church continues to dictate governance over women's lives and bodies, through its stance on abortion and birth control, and its refusal to offer women equal opportunities in religious callings, such as the priesthood. It is unacceptable to me that a woman must dress modestly and cover her head so as not to tempt men, to show deference to her husband and her God, when a man is not likewise required to do this. That men believe they are entitled to control the lives of women under the guise of dogma is infuriating. But covering, like so many beliefs, is wrapped up in religious and cultural values that make it complicated to unravel.

In 2010 I moved further into the Muslim world when I accepted a teaching job in the United Arab Emirates. In the classroom all the women were covered, and the classes were single sex and held on separate campuses of the same school. If there were the occasional shocking stories of honour killings in Turkey, the reality in the UAE was that there were no opportunities for young women and men to mingle prior to marriage. Women were held to a strict dress code of covering themselves at all times while in public in both the black *abaya* gown and the *shayla* head scarf. A few girls were covered more thoroughly than others. Some covered their face and in a few cases their hands as well. When I looked out at my class I occasionally saw women who resembled the nuns I grew up with, and I was reminded that even the Catholic Church eventually allowed nuns to uncover.

After five years in the UAE I have learned more about the intertwining of culture, family, and religion. While some girls are allowed to cut their hair short and, at least around school, wear their *shaylas* around their neck rather than tightly over their heads, most girls keep their hair covered at all times. They generally cannot have their picture taken if it is going to be seen publicly, and they are not permitted to be alone in public, or make independent decisions. If they come from a more conservative family, a brother (younger or older) has authority over them. For example, although women may drive and many do, if a father, brother or husband forbids it, then they do not drive, no matter how old they are. A father once explained to me that daughters are precious and must be protected, which is the reason for the *abaya* and *shayla*. On the other hand, many girls say the *abaya* and *shayla* are the national dress and they are proud to wear it. And, too, there are girls who openly say they wished they did not have to wear any of it, but they must.

With that said, Emirati women are far more uncovered and free in their covered state than many of the other Muslim women from other countries who also live in the UAE and are more heavily covered. Under their flowing *abayas* many of the Emirati girls are wearing jeans, sleeveless tops, and stiletto heels, and their makeup is exquisitely executed. And when they step out in public and pull the veil down over their entire face, it doesn't always look like a forced retreat from the world, but rather like privacy from the world.

In the UAE, and in Muslim countries generally, culture and religion are interwoven, and it is not always clear which are the laws of the land and which are the laws of God (or laws of men speaking on behalf of God). Muslim countries are primarily collectivist societies in which the extended family group is of primary importance, and it matters what the neighbours think. It is the women as much as the men who monitor and enforce cultural and religious behaviour, and children are raised to accept without dissent the rules governing what is proper behaviour and what is forbidden in the community. For this reason, it is far more common for religious values to be incorporated into and accepted at the civic level because these are viewed as one and the same. There was a time when the Catholic Church also held sway over all aspects of the daily lives of people, but that time is long past. The separation of church and state is now demanded by the majority of people in Christian-dominated countries. Families may impose religious practices on children, but communities recognize the freedom of those children to choose differently when they reach adulthood.

The challenge of having a secular Muslim state is that when the majority of the population is Muslim, there is a strong persuasion towards shared religious and cultural values. People want those values validated by their leaders, which is to say that what is good from an Islamic values perspective should be agreed upon as good for the whole community. Thus, a separation is not desired and secular Muslim states are not prevalent. And when the leadership of the religion is dominated by men, and men believe that it is their right to say what is proper behaviour for women, women continue to have a subservient and obedient role in society, and transgressions are met with varying degrees of severity.

Many women believe that covering their heads is a valued tradition of Muslim women, whether cultural or religious, and they *want* to do this. It is not my place to argue and certainly not to suggest that it should be forbidden. What is complicated is that it is so difficult for head covering to be left to choice. The more it is visible in public, the more it is accepted as the correct behaviour of the community, and the more unacceptable it becomes to choose to not cover. And though the Prophet did not say that women must be covered, he did insist that his own wives be covered as protection from men, rather than insisting that men take responsibility for their own behaviour. As a result, Muslim women often believe they are emulating the conduct of the good wives of the Prophet, when those women did not themselves have the choice.

With that said, when I opened the envelope from my Turkish student who went to America, I burst out laughing at the photograph she had sent me of herself. There she was on the last night at the international student dinner wearing a big smile and a great big sombrero hat on her head — over her scarf, of course. She was happy, and I was happy for her. It's a complicated issue.

Scarves
Dragana Randelovic

> *"Everything you see is a reflection of itself.*
> *You move around and you are a reflection of what is next to you."*
> ~Grace Paleg

My first experience with covered women is from my childhood in Serbia. At that time, whenever I visited my grandparents in the countryside near my hometown of Nis, my grandma was the one who was always waiting for us at the welcoming gate, her hair covered by a colourful scarf. The scarves she wore were a blend of different hues and designs to match her clothes. As I never saw my granny dressed in light colours, my memory of her is reflected in shades of navy, brown, grey, burgundy or purple. These were the colours of her scarves as well.

When I started primary school in the 1980s I would spend my summer holidays at my grandparents' house. I remember my granny at home *sans* the scarf while she did housework, but as soon as she heard the doorbell she would put it on to welcome her guests. I also remember her comments at that time. "Oh we have visitors and I'm not covered. Shame on me." So wearing a scarf in front of guests and neighbours was normal for me.

Then one day something interesting happened. I was five years old and I remember getting ready to go to my uncle's wedding party. Everyone was busy running around. There was so much to do. In the middle of all the hubbub, my granny turned to my mom and said, "Make an appointment with the hairdresser, please. I have to do my hair. It's a shame to cover my hair for my son's wedding!"

This confused me. That's probably why I still remember it. I wondered why every woman in the village wore a scarf in public and it was a "shame" if they didn't have it on, but at the same time, whenever there was a celebration, it was a "shame" if they did have it on! I knew that some of the wedding guests would be her neighbours—the same neighbours for whom she would cover her hair before meeting them at the door—but my granny didn't seem to mind if they saw her scarf-less at the event.

My grandma (on the right) with her brother and sister-in-law.
Photo courtesy of Dragana Randelovic

Although I was confused at the time, I realize now that this dichotomy not only applied to my granny's case. It was clearly a custom that was accepted in my country during that time. Even now, when I look at pictures from my childhood in the countryside, I rarely find one in which the grandmothers are wearing scarves. At birthday parties, weddings and various events, the photos show women with short, tidy hair and no headscarves in sight. Even in photographs, this was a common custom. Of course, unlike today with its Facebook, Instagram and selfie mania, people in my grandmother's time weren't photographed very often, so that in itself was a special occasion. And as with any special event, the women would take off their scarves and comb their hair before shooting.

When I was younger, the headscarf was part of the everyday life of rural women in Serbia. At one time I thought that the scarves served to cover unwashed and untidy hair. As women in the countryside spent a lot of time in the field, they weren't always able to nurture long hair and beautiful hairstyles, so the scarf was useful in public. Also in the cold winter days the scarves would protect them from the chilling temperatures.

Women in Serbian village.
Photo courtesy of Dragana Randelovic

Another interesting fact that I began to think about when I grew up is that both of my grannies lived in the city when they got married and while they raised their children. Later, when their children were settled, they moved back to the countryside home where they were born. While living in the city they never wore headscarves. Instead, they went regularly to the hairdresser and had beautiful hair. Later, when they moved back to the village, they began to wear headscarves. Was this because of their age or the environment in which they were living? As it turns out, age had very little to do with my granny's headscarf.

I learned this after my grandfather's death when my granny moved back to the city to live with my family. Immediately she took off her headscarf. She was around 70 years old at the time, but wearing a headscarf in the city was simply considered old-fashioned.

There are several explanations of the tradition of wearing headscarves in my region of the world. Reflecting the religious aspect, the root of this tradition lies in Christianity. We can find in the Bible a sentence that states, "And every woman who prays to God with her head uncovered dishonours her head." (Corinthians 11:3) In the previous century, this adage was particularly effective to ensure that women covered their heads when visiting monasteries and churches. The tradition eventually wore away in Serbia, so today it's usually only the elderly women who have their head covered when entering a place of worship. In Russia, however, where people practise the same Russian Orthodox religion as we do in Serbia, that tradition is preserved to this day. Women do not enter holy places without headscarves.

Traditional Serbian dress
Photo courtesy of Dragana Randelovic

If we look at this phenomenon from an historical point of view we can say that the tradition of wearing headscarves in the Serbian region was not only influenced by Christian doctrine, but also by the religious and cultural norms of the rulers. Central and Southern Serbia and Bosnia spent five hundred years as part of the Ottoman Empire, which left a huge impact on our culture, customs, and cuisine. The headscarf is one of the remnants of the influence of Islamic culture during the 500 years of Ottoman rule. Bosnian Serbs under Turkish occupation often accepted Islam to avoid suffering various consequences of not doing so. These are now the Bosnians who speak the Serbian language but follow Islam rather than Christianity. Considering that both Bosnia and Serbia used to be united as part of the country of Yugoslavia, it is only natural for Muslim traditions such as the headscarf to be a part of Serbian customs.

In today's cultural climate, the headscarf seems to evoke many negative feelings among Europeans. For me, the concept of a woman in a headscarf has never provoked any negative sentiments. I grew up with this custom, seeing it as a regular habit of my granny's. Plus, when I was small, I spent a lot of time travelling with my family around the part of Yugoslavia that is now Bosnia, so seeing Muslim women in headscarves was normal for me.

Throughout my life, I have had numerous experiences that have made the headscarf even more acceptable for me. In the period of my earliest childhood, there were many citizens of Iraq, Syria and Jordan who were studying in Serbia, especially in my hometown. My family had a big house, so we used some of the apartments to accommodate these male students. As the students were just a few years younger than my parents, they used to spend a lot of time with us. For the first ten years of my life, these people were present every day in our home. They became an extended part of my family. As a child, I was very curious, so I used to listen to stories about Baghdad and Damascus, about their culture, custom, and textiles. I enjoyed looking at the photos of their mothers and sisters wearing colourful dresses and headscarves. So when I visited Syria as a university student, the headscarves were just another charm of the country. To be honest, seeing a covered woman on the streets of Syria didn't attract my attention at all. It was just normal, like seeing a woman wearing a scarf in the rural parts of Serbia.

A few years ago, I moved from Serbia to the United Arab Emirates. Now, you would think that the sea of headscarves in Abu Dhabi would make no impression on me whatsoever. After all, scarves were a natural part of being a woman for so many of the people I had grown up with. So, why was it that I felt an unnatural anxiety when seeing so many women covered in black? It truly bothered me. For a long time, I couldn't understand the emotional response I was having. Was it the headscarf or was it something else?

Funeral in Serbia
Photo courtesy of Dragana Randelovic

In my country black is the color of pain and sadness. After the death of a family member or loved one, the custom in Serbia is to wear black clothes for the next forty days, six months, one year, or even three years. How long you wear black depends on the relationship you had with the deceased person and the intensity of your pain and sorrow. At the funerals of husbands or family members, women are dressed completely in black and wear black headscarves. The black *abayas* and scarves that are customary for women in the Emirates and other Gulf countries reminded me of these Serbian funerals. For the first few months, I felt completely engulfed by the grief which I always associated with the ensemble. Every time I would see these women, I had feelings of fear, pain and sadness.

Today, after living in Abu Dhabi for the past four years, my eyes and my mind have become accustomed to the flutter of dark robes in the bright sunshine. That which I associated only with death has now become a part of everyday life. As a result of seeing the black *abayas* on the streets, in the malls, and in all the public spaces, I no longer fear them. In fact, I see now the pride and elegance with which the Emirati women carry themselves. This is what they are communicating with their dress.

I know that what is normal in one part of the world can be completely foreign in another. I needed to spend time in the UAE to understand the emotional responses I was having to my surroundings. Since the colourful headscarves were a part of my experience growing up, they never elicited any strong reactions. Once I became acclimatised to the culture of the Emirates, my own interpretation of the blackness faded away. I began to notice the gentle flow of the black robes and the slightly flirty way in which the scarf is wrapped and rewrapped around a woman's head.

Fear, I think, comes from a place that is so deep inside us that we don't want to go near it, but sometimes the best way to overcome our fears, especially those that we cannot rationalize, is to face them head on. The black headscarves and *abayas* are normal in Abu Dhabi, so I could not run away from them. I had to deal with my feelings. Perhaps this is what is lacking in a lot of places these days. We run away from all the things we don't understand. We dehumanize people that don't look like us or behave like us. If they – the "others" — are few in number and we are the many, we can do this and feel empowered. But really, we are not empowered when we act out of fear. We are merely little children hiding under the covers, afraid of the monster under the bed or in the wardrobe. So when I read about all the negative incidents in different parts of Europe surrounding the headscarf, I wonder more about the people who fear it, rather than those who wear it.

To Hijab or Not To Hijab
Reverend Nell Green

*"Travel is fatal to prejudice, bigotry, and narrow-mindedness, and many
of our people need it sorely on these accounts. Broad, wholesome, charitable
views of men and things cannot be acquired by vegetating in one little corner
of the earth all one's lifetime."*
~Mark Twain

I am a Baptist by choice, not by tradition. I came to the Baptist Protestant
Church when I was a senior in high school. What attracted me, besides my
decision to be a follower of Christ, was the autonomy of the local church and
the freedom of each believer to decide what they believed based on scripture —
sola scriptura, as it was called by those men and women who began the
Reformation. Yet even these early reformers encouraged women to cover their
hair, particularly in church. Covering the head demonstrated submission to
men, who were the "head of woman", according to some interpretations of the
New Testament. Some women went so far as to keep it covered when sleeping
and bathing. Eventually the practice became limited to church attendance
where a woman's head was required to be covered when she prayed or spoke.
As women became more independent of men in Europe and North America,
this practice eventually fell by the wayside for many Protestant churches,
particularly Baptists. Many Christian women still see men as their authority
and many still feel a need to cover their head and not teach men in church.
While this is not how I practise my Protestant faith, I respect their desire to
follow Christ according to their interpretation of scripture.

As a follower of Christ, I sensed a calling as a young woman to serve others.
This mission brought me to many parts of the world. I left for my first overseas
assignment in 1986. The women of the Muslim country where I first served,
Senegal, wore head coverings. It actually had little to do with faith expression
or modesty and more to do with style. And style they did! While I could not
make as elaborate a headdress as my friends, I nevertheless enjoyed wearing
them and showing off my own sense of style. The women of Senegal were known
for their beauty, and their headdresses, and long robes (*boubous*) contributed
to that.

129

Wearing the boubous in Senegal
Photo courtesy of Nell Green

A few years later, I lived in an area of Brussels, Belgium, that was made up primarily of Muslims from North Africa. Their hijab had everything to do with modesty and expressing their faith. I realized that going out one rainy afternoon when I put on my rain coat and a scarf for protection. That day, three different friends asked me if I had converted to Islam! They assumed that wearing the scarf was an outward expression of my faith. It was my first introduction to the significance of hijab for my Muslim friends. I understood and respected their desire and their right to hijab, but until then I had not connected it with an open affiliation to Islam.

When a dear friend decided that she would wear hijab continuously, I began to realize just how popular and controversial that choice was becoming among my Muslim friends. Previously she had covered only when men were present.

When she began to wear it continuously, one of our mutual Christian friends expressed her disappointment that she had "regressed" and "moved backwards" rather than forward. Upon hearing this sentiment, my Muslim friend became teary-eyed. "I just want to go deeper in my devotion to Allah."

I understood and supported her desire to wear her hijab. However, the situation was different a few months later when this same Muslim friend found out that her new sister-in-law preferred not to hijab. "Well, no worries about that!" she proclaimed. "We will put enough pressure on her that in three months she will be wearing it." And indeed, within three months, her sister-in-law was wearing the scarf.

When I returned to Brussels some years later for a visit, I gathered with my friend. Her sisters and her daughter were also present that afternoon. Previously, when we were all together, the sisters would leave their hair uncovered. However, on this occasion, each one of the women, including my friend's daughter, was wearing the hijab. I remembered the remark that my friend had made about her sister-in-law, and I couldn't help but wonder if it was their own choice to cover or if it was on account of pressure from the family.

In Europe, hijab is often seen as an offensive outward expression of faith that contributes to barriers between people. Governments still argue over the practice in schools and public places. I think it is important to note that such sentiments do not necessarily single out Muslims alone. In Belgium my own children were not allowed to wear a cross or a t-shirt which expressed their faith. When it came to hijab, the barrier that was most visible to me was the one between men and women. As a woman, I knew of the appropriateness of distance between men and women in Islamic cultures. Hijab helped create that distance. Yet, as a woman who valued her equality with men and her freedom, I realized that I was beginning to resent it. It seemed one more way that women were set apart. Don't shake hands with a man. Don't smile at a man. Don't look a man in the eyes. Don't have your hair uncovered in front of a man.

I do international fashion shows called "Global Runways" in which I use authentic garments representing different cultures from around the world. Rather than a typical fashion show, however, as the garments are modelled I explain the cultural, political, social plights of the women from that particular part of the world. My goal is to help the audience understand that the person they look at and perhaps think "dresses weird" is a normal person just like them. If they will look past the dress and other differences, then forming a relationship becomes possible. During one particular event, I wore an authentic Afghani *burka*. Unlike other garments from Muslim cultures, I felt completely walled off in the *burka*. It was difficult for me to get my message of diversity across. No one knew it was me and no one would engage in even the most mundane conversation with me. It became clear to me then what some Muslim women must feel when they are veiled so fully.

My personal moment of reckoning, however, came one afternoon after we had moved stateside. My husband and I were joining Muslim friends for a celebration to be held in the local mosque. As we left, my husband asked if I had my scarf. I told him of course I did. When we arrived at the mosque, he asked me again if I had my scarf. I realized that his questioning was making me resentful. "What business is it of his?" I thought. "I know what I need. What I don't need is my husband overseeing my dress!" Since we practise equality in our marriage, I realized that for me the scarf was turning into an object of authority and oppression.

Among my Muslim friends and neighbours, however, hijab was hardly questioned. Girls wore them to school. Women wore them to work. One Muslim woman explained that at the office she felt it made her less of a sexual object. Hijab helped her be heard and respected. Another woman, however, said that she felt Americans either ignored her at best or excluded her at worse, because hijab set her apart. None of my new friends said they felt persecuted just because they wore it. Even today, when I go to the store in my current city of Houston, over half the women have their head covered. I go to watch a high school basketball game and a few of the female players have long pants and hijab. Perhaps it is because of the ethnic and religious diversity of the city, but wearing hijab in Houston seems like a non-issue. It's just another part of the life here.

I recently went to a country in the Middle East where hijab is required. It should be noted that hijab is not mandatory in most Muslim-majority countries. I have been to multiple countries in the region that did not require me to cover, particularly if it was obvious I was not from there. After we had landed in the country, my scarf slipped off quite accidentally. The flight attendant ran down the aisle and implored me quickly to move it back into place. It scared me to death. "Really, a simple scarf?" I thought to myself. "A

simple slip and we should all be scared to the point of tears and racing hearts?"
Truthfully, at the end of my ten day visit, I could not wait to take it off.

In front of Persepolis in Iran
Photo courtesy of Nell Green

I completely respect my Muslim friends' desire for and right to hijab. I advocate for it to be their choice and not that of the society surrounding them. I venerate their right even as I wish to be respected for my expressions of faith, such as wearing a cross. I do not wish to be judged as immodest because I do not cover my hair, or because I choose to wear a tank top or pants that might appear tight in someone else's view. In the same way, I do not wish for my Muslim friends to be judged and possibly rejected by either their own society or their host society because they exercise their choice to dress as they please. While I understand we all view the relationship between men and women differently, I advocate for equality for my Muslim women friends. I advocate for them to be free of pressure from strangers, from governments, and even from their own friends and families.

I advocate for their right to decide whether to hijab or not to hijab.

PART 3

CHOICES IN BELONGING

Who Am I?
Fawzia Mai Tung

> *"When I discover who I am, I'll be free."*
> ~Ralph Ellison, *Invisible Man*

Soon after 9/11, stories about attacks on Muslims popped up in the news, and subsequently a number of female friends and acquaintances here in the US removed their hijabs. My husband grew concerned too. One day, he asked me if I should also consider removing it.

"No," I told him. "I never even thought about it."

Some people asked me where I found the courage and strength to keep it on. Strength? Courage? I had never thought about it that way.

I remember a chat I had in Jeddah with a number of Chinese sisters who all wore the black veil while in Saudi, but removed it when on holiday in Taiwan. They all mentioned how difficult it was to meet everyone's stares and questions. It was much easier just to dress like everyone else and melt in the crowd. Indeed, one of the universal biggest fears is public speaking, and I imagine that dressing yourself in a markedly different way is similar to public speaking. Everyone's eyes are on you. You are always on a stage - in the streets, the stores, the offices, everywhere.

I had made the decision to put on the hijab shortly before marriage, when I still lived in Jeddah, then wore it on my travels to Singapore, Hong Kong, Taiwan, Japan, and the US, where I got married. It was 1984, and the trendiest look at the time was an Egyptian style made up of two pieces of very light fabric. It involved twisting a long braid around the top of the head and slipping the second piece to form a beautiful falling fold. In keeping with the fashion, I purchased scarves in a dozen different colours to match my clothes. The style looked great except that it was very tight, and by the end of the day, I always ended up with flattened hair and a headache.

I remember in Singapore, as I was walking down the street, three young ladies came up to me and asked, "This thing you are wearing on your head, is it for fashion or for religion?" To which I answered, it was both. I suppose there were enough Muslims in Singapore for them to ask that so freely. But in Taiwan, I would get a totally different type of question. "Are you from Mongolia or from

Tibet?" Or, from a slightly more knowledgeable person, "Are you from Malaysia?" It would totally stun them when I'd answer that I was from Taiwan, just like they were.

In the office of a family acquaintance, the young Taiwanese secretary stared at my pink flowing hijab for a long time and then said to me, "Can I tell you something? This thing you are wearing is actually not making you more beautiful!"

My immediate reaction was to burst into laughter. When I regained my composure, I kindly informed her that I was not wearing it in order to look more beautiful, but to cover my beauty. I still giggle today when I recall her facial expression.

Some time after my marriage in the US, we moved again to Jeddah, and it was there that the question of courage popped up. In my mind, I rewound the video of my life and saw that, indeed, I had never had any problem appearing in front of either acquaintances or strangers wearing the hijab. No embarrassment whatsoever. Instead, I had been proud and willing to share information about my faith and my practice. This new me – the *muhajjabah* – was starkly different from the shy and inhibited little girl I used to be many years ago.

How did this happen?

My father was a diplomat, and consequently I followed him all over the world in an era when there weren't any international schools. In 1959, my elder sister and I were enrolled in a French public "maternelle" (preschool and kindergarten). Not many people had television and, even so, there weren't any Chinese faces on TV. So we were a great exotic spectacle to our schoolmates. During recess, the children would form a large circle around the two of us, and pull the outer corners of their eyes up, then flatten their noses, and chant, "Oh la chinoise! Oh la chinoise!" Oh, the Chinese girl! Oh, the Chinese girl!

Well, it wasn't exactly enjoyable for a three-year-old and so I'd scream my heart out every morning when my mother dropped me off to school. I would grab her dress and refuse to let go while hollering at the top of my voice. She would push me and Mme Mireille, my teacher, would pull me, until my fingers were pried open. This little scene would repeat itself every day. I hated having a little flat nose and slanted Chinese eyes and "yellow" skin. My parents told me that "phoenix eyes" in China are rare and considered beautiful. It certainly did not feel so in school, and so I hated them.

In my dreams, I had porcelain white skin, blue eyes and blonde hair, but in the morning I would wake in the same skin, with the same eyes, the same nose. Of course, there is nothing a child can do about her physical attributes. It is not something you can decide to wear or not to wear. It was something I was born with, and I had to accept it, like it or not.

We moved to Ankara, Turkey, in 1964. There, I was fortunate to attend the French embassy school which accepted international students. I loved the fact that my schoolmates were French, Turkish, American, Vietnamese, Polish and just about every shade and colour under the sun. No one minded my skin, my nose, my eyes or my hair. Unfortunately, this happiness did not last long. A year later, my father was transferred again, this time to Jeddah, Saudi Arabia.

We finished the year at the Chinese embassy school, which was a one-room school with twelve children of all ages and grades, like something out of *Little House on the Prairie* or *Anne of Green Gables*. All the students were Chinese and all the teachers were parents. My father was the principal and the English teacher; my mother taught music. We also took Arabic, maths and Mandarin. It was wonderful! But alas, this too did not last. The next school year, my father changed the embassy school to just a half day in the afternoon, and enrolled us at the closest Saudi elementary school for girls. Saudi Arabia had just started opening girls' schools a few years earlier, and this one was built on an old cemetery, and staffed with Egyptian teachers.

The first day of school, we arrived too early. So my sister and I sat on a wooden bench, in our uniform grey dresses, white socks and black shoes, waiting for assembly to start. Soon the girls started filling up the school yard, and a crowd grew around us. They pushed and shoved and pointed fingers, chattering excitedly. The wall of students was so thick you couldn't put a finger through. The two of us just pretended nothing was happening and sat on, stoically. Eventually, I bent toward my sister's ear, and whispered in French (for that was our primary tongue), "I feel like I'm in a circus..."

I thought our bench was against the wall, but there was actually some space between the bench and the wall. The crowd had become so dense that some girls had squeezed themselves into that space and one of them had stuck her ear between our heads when I spoke those fateful words. She immediately tried imitating the sound of what she thought was Chinese, loudly and clownishly, for the benefit of the crowd, "ching chang ching chang ching chang...!" Raucous laughter erupted and rolled over the entire yard.

By then I knew the futility of trying to avoid school and never even broached the subject with my parents. Eventually, the crowd thinned out day by day, but some particularly curious girls would not stop having some fun at our expense. Groups or pairs of girls would stop by us daily and ask, "Aish ismik?" (what is your name?) and we would dutifully answer, "Saadia wa Fawzia...", which would send them into fits of laughter, probably because we had such an unusual accent. We finally stopped telling them our names, because it was obvious the entire school knew already, and the question was not aimed at getting to know us. One girl would come and snatch away my handkerchief, which we had to have laundered and ironed in our pocket, supposedly for cleaning our nose, but really for inspection at any time. She'd run a little and stop, and wave it at me. "Come and get it!" In those days, the stress of schooling had given me a peptic ulcer and I was pretty much just skin and bones and very weak. I would try to run awkwardly, feel faint, and start crying.

Two years later, my uncle was transferred to Paris as the Taiwan representative at UNESCO. My parents decided that Saadia and I were wasting our education in Jeddah and sent us to live with my aunt (my mother's sister). Back in France, we found ourselves more than three years ahead of our peers in French literature, grammar, vocabulary and spelling. This was because during our stay in Jeddah we had spent all our spare time reading and re-reading my father's shelves, which were filled with French classics. The Chinese maths had also worked its wonders, so we were doing pretty well in school, always coming first.

Getting good grades had always given me some measure of respect from teachers and classmates, so I imagined that this time, with French girls much older and wiser, I would not encounter the type of discrimination and bullying I had to put up with in my earlier childhood. For a while, I really thought it was so. Then one day, during my third year in Paris, at a private Catholic girls school run by nuns, I found out I had only been fooling myself.

The history teacher was returning our monthly tests. In those days in France, a history test would be something like, "Describe the life of a common Roman citizen under the reign of Emperor Augustus." Then you would have to fill up five pages. There weren't any multiple choice or fill-in-the-blank type questions. She had returned everyone's paper except mine. She stopped, and to the whole class, she announced, "I want to tell you all that in my whole career as a history teacher, I have never given a full mark to anyone. Ever. But I did this month. The answer was so complete there was nothing I could find missing. Can you guess who it is?"

Since I had not received my paper back yet, I knew it must be me. I felt flushed with happiness and embarrassment. At which point, an acidic voice, something between a sneer and a curse, piped somewhere to my right, behind me, "Oh... we know very well... it is that little Chinese... c'est la p'tite chinoise, la!"

I felt my face grow cold, and my eyes nearly gushed with tears. I tried very hard to control them, and make my eyes swallow them back in. I hated my perfect score and wished I had never gotten it. Life went on, and I continued to attend school with my Chinese face and my good scores, antagonizing my French classmates.

The year after, my uncle was transferred to Geneva. My parents and other siblings had been back in Taiwan for a year already, so they decided it was time for Saadia and me to come home. I was on cloud nine. Finally, I'd be among my own kind. I would not stand out like a sore thumb anymore!

While I had excelled at the school in France, in Taipei my grades were terrible. My Chinese was barely second grade level, and we were then in ninth grade. This was the year in which junior high school students prepared to take the national exam for entrance into senior high school, so apart from the actual curriculum, we had to review everything from seventh and eighth grades, plus keep taking mock national exams.

We started school in Taipei two weeks late, so we were introduced to our class one bright morning, standing in front of all of them. There were 57 of us in one classroom and I was number 57. I sat through our first class and understood very little. The teacher wrote notes on the blackboard, and I couldn't read the notes. The Chinese I had learned was from textbooks, printed clearly, so I had learned to print my characters just like that. But by middle school, students would write in a script that was hasty and simplified, rather like today's simplified characters in China, but even more rounded and flowing. So I stared at the board and wondered what those words were. My deskmate (we sat two to a desk) kindly copied them for me in my book, but that wasn't any use because

I still couldn't read them.

Then, at the end of class, the teacher told us verbally what the homework was. I glanced furtively around. No one was writing it down! What to do? In France, we had a planner with color-coded days of the week in which we wrote down all our homework and its due dates. Somehow, all Chinese students simply memorized what they were supposed to do. I couldn't. I pulled out the notebook I'd brought with me but, afraid others would wonder what I was up to, I kept it on my lap, and proceeded to write in French what the teacher had just said. No sooner had I started writing than a voice behind me sneered semi-loudly, "What a show off! She's trying to show off that she can write in English!"

It was then that I realized it: try as I may, I did not belong in Taiwan either. I had turned into a strange animal, not belonging here nor there, an alien wherever I went. To be fair, I did pick up a lot of pride in Chinese culture and history and carried that with me when we moved to Jordan two years later.

Coming of age in Amman was liberating, for Jordan boasts a mix of ethnicities and religions. Though there were barely any Chinese in those days in Amman, and I was consequently the target of finger-pointing and stares in the streets, I had become by then immune to these. Learning taekwondo boosted my self-confidence. It was Bruce Lee who came to my rescue, when his movies burst onto the entertainment scene and took Jordan by storm. The kids in the street suddenly looked up to us, now calling out, "Bruce Lee! Bruce Lee!" when we walked around. They recognized our shared ethnicity and no longer looked down on us. I wasn't sure how I felt, being identified as a martial arts expert, rather than a yellow monkey. But one thing had not changed - I was still an outsider.

Adolescence was a time when I wrestled with self-identity, a time when I poured out poems by the dozen, usually written in the middle of the night. I would stare at the moon and tell her that the night was my homeland. It was during my days as a medical student and an intern that I finally re-discovered my own religion, Islam. My home was now the entire earth, and my compatriots were all the Muslims in the world. How I came to wear the hijab is a long story, one that maybe I will tell elsewhere. Essentially, I loved the feeling of protection it gave me, protection from prying eyes, protection from intrusion.

Fast forward to 9/11...

I now lived in the US where Asian faces were common and no one stared at my features for whatever reason. However, some would glare at my scarf. I had experienced my share of grouchy cashiers at the check-out counter who would greet the customer before and after me with friendliness. But that barely bothered me.

I had by then worn the hijab for about fifteen years and had evolved beyond the original two-piece chiffon to just a plain square cotton scarf folded into a triangle, much easier for a busy mother of seven. It was a choice, something I could discard any minute, not something stuck to me like my skin colour and the shape of my eyes and nose. I could choose to join the world of anonymity and melt in the crowd of women in modern t-shirts and jeans, with the breeze blowing softly through their hair.

But I did not.

And I did not quite figure out why for a long time – until I was asked about it.

Courage? Strength? It had nothing to do with any of these. It became obvious to me that this is who I am - a righteous Muslim woman. Wearing the hijab advertises that fact to the world loud and clear. And so, it is as impossible for me to remove it.

As impossible as it is to peel off my skin or my nose.

Confessions of a Confused *Muhajjabah*
T. Akhtar

"I believe more follies are committed out of complaisance to the world,
than in following our own inclinations."
~Mary Wortley

When I was asked to write something about my thoughts on hijab, I thought I wouldn't have much to say. I wear the hijab and though it might not have started out as something I did by choice, it has become ingrained into my life. It is like a habit that is hard to break. The first time that I ever consciously thought about why I was doing it was when I started writing this narrative. The more I thought about it, the more confused I became.

I was born and raised in Karachi, Pakistan in a typical middle class household. We lived in what is called a joint family, which basically means that my grandmother, unmarried aunts and my paternal uncle's family all lived with us in one big house. Both my parents worked and I had the best childhood that anyone could have. My family never differentiated between boys and girls, and I grew up believing myself to be as good, if not better, than the boys. I played with boys on the streets, went out with friends and generally had an upbringing in which every child was encouraged to be independent and find their own paths in life.

I always dressed in what I thought was a conservative manner, which meant that my shoulders and legs were covered. Head covering was never an issue, neither was the length of my sleeves. My grandmother used to wear a *burka* (similar to an *abaya* with a face veil), but her sons made her get rid of it when we were kids. I wore jeans and t-shirts as much as I wore *shalwar kameez*, the traditional Pakistani dress, with a scarf around my neck. Looking back, maybe I lived with people who were tolerant and not opinionated about what a girl wore or did. Later on, I would realize that there were people in the world who not only thought about it, but had the power to alter my whole appearance.

I was always a keen reader, a trait that my brothers and I inherited from both our parents. My school had an extensive library and a British librarian who encouraged my love for books. I mention this here because I was in no way sheltered from the way of life in other parts of the world. My dress growing up

144

was completely my own choice, but much influenced by my upbringing in a Pakistani Muslim household. In those days during the 1980s and the 1990s, being a Muslim didn't immediately conjure up images of *burka* clad women and bearded men.

My husband and I met as students in the same university. He knew who I was when he decided to marry me. He had to go through a bit of a struggle because he belonged to a community in which no one married an outsider. But, my in-laws were good people and he eventually won their approval. They were more open-minded than most of the other people in their community, but not by much. My family, by contrast, was happy with my choice, although everyone kept warning me about the conservative mindset I was marrying into.

This isn't a story about the hardships that I had to face because, to be honest, there weren't many. Everyone has to go through an adjustment period after marriage and so did I. Yes, there were huge differences, and yes, it was sometimes difficult, but both sides were committed to making it work. My husband lived in a joint family with his parents and two younger brothers. While my husband has never to date dictated anything about the way I dress, my mother-in-law made it clear from the beginning that when I was with her I was supposed to cover myself with a *chador*. A *chador* is like a big sheet of cloth that covers the head and goes down to below the hips. My mother-in-law herself wears an *abaya* and has been wearing it for some time now. It was not a big deal for me, since I only had to cover myself while outside and there was no such restriction in the house. During the next three years I became used to the *chador*. It started feeling like a natural mode of dress while out in the market or other public places. My life had changed completely and for the first time I became uncomfortable with the way some men stared at women on the streets of Karachi. My *chador* made me feel protected from these stares and so it became a part of me.

In December 2006, my husband and I went for Hajj, the Muslim pilgrimage to Mecca. Let me explain here the context of modest covering as accepted by most scholars of Islam. A woman is supposed to cover herself from neck to wrists and ankles and avoid any show of skin. It is above the neck that the scholars cannot agree upon. Some say that a woman has to cover all of herself with just an opening for the eyes; others say that covering the face is not compulsory and it is acceptable to just cover the head; still others say that covering the head is not mentioned anywhere in the Quran and modest dressing is up to the interpretation of an individual. Actually, it all depends on the sect that one follows. There are many sects in Islam and, while the basics are the same, some concepts are interpreted differently by each sect.

When we decided to go for Hajj, I took a decision that, while in Saudi Arabia, I would wear an *abaya* and a scarf, but I would not cover my face. I had no intention of continuing to wear the *abaya* after coming back. However, as soon as everyone found out about our going, pressure started building from my in-laws' side. Both my mother-in-law and sister-in-law wore *abayas* and they started telling me how I should keep wearing it after I came back. Reluctantly, I acquiesced and started wearing the *abaya*. I didn't want to do it and I should have realized that I wasn't up for it when I started ditching the *abaya* anytime my in-laws weren't around. In some instances it came in handy, like when going to pick up my son from school. I didn't have to change and could just put on the *abaya* and go. But essentially, I wore the *abaya* in Pakistan to keep my in-laws happy.

It was then that the hypocrisy of the situation became apparent. The whole concept of a woman covering herself is there to keep her hidden from the eyes of men not directly related to her. In other words, a woman can uncover her head in front of men directly related to her, like her father, brother, maternal/ paternal uncles, husband and father-in-law, all those relations whom she's not allowed to marry. According to this belief, if I were covering my head while outside, I was also supposed to do it in the house in front of my brothers-in-law, my servants and other men apart from my husband and my father-in-law. So, I started covering my head while at home because it followed the lines of logic. I thought it was the right thing to do, considering the level of religious covering that I was constantly being pressured to uphold. But to my surprise, this did not find favour with my mother-in-law! She kept saying that I didn't need to do it at home as they were all family!

In 2010, my husband and I moved to Dubai with our children. It was another world for me. There was no pressure to conform to anyone's rules, interpretations or perspectives, and for the first time in my life I was free to do as I pleased. I continued wearing my *abaya* for a while until I realized that I couldn't stand the heat. I had to walk to pick up my son from school, and the weather in Dubai made it difficult to wear layers. I put away the *abaya* and started going out wearing my *shalwar kameez* and *dupatta*. The *dupatta* is again, a type of scarf, but longer, and can be worn on the head without any pins or just used to cover the chest. I opted for wearing it on my head. Without realizing it, I had become used to covering my head!

Slowly I came back to wearing jeans and long skirts. When I first got married, I had had to wear the traditional *shalwar kameez* at all times. This was again in keeping with my in-laws' wishes. It was not that much of a sacrifice then as I had never been too fond of dressing up anyway and could make do with just about anything. In Dubai, it dawned on me that I could wear whatever I wanted! I could be just another person on the street and no one would care what I had on. What I didn't know was that, as I had studied a bit of religion, it had left its mark on me. I was now uncomfortable wearing anything other than full sleeves, and felt more comfortable when I was covering my head.

And that is how I started wearing the hijab.

It has now been three years in Dubai, and I continue to cover my hair. It was never a conscious decision. I think I'm just more at ease this way. I honestly cannot condemn someone for not covering her head, nor can I preach to others what I myself am not sure about. My decision had nothing to do with religion. I'm actually not the most religious person that you will meet. I still have best friends who are males. I still stay out late with friends. I still gossip and bitch about people. There have been instances when people have stereotyped me because of the way I dress and then have received the surprise of their lives when they come to know me better. People keep expecting me to discuss religion and be preachy, while I prefer to run away from such topics.

Still, the hijab stays a part of me — sometimes in the form of a scarf, sometimes a *dupatta*, and sometimes as an *abaya*. But I live in Dubai, a city of paradoxes where hijab is as normal as a miniskirt. Would I still be wearing the hijab if I were living somewhere in, say, Europe where I might have to face some serious discrimination because of it? I find it increasingly difficult to answer that question.

Lately, I have begun to get a bit annoyed with it too. I sometimes get the urge to wear nice earrings or style my hair in a certain way, and I know that I cannot do it because I cover my head. Sometimes, I feel that my face looks fat in a hijab and no matter what I might say, I'm still a woman, and there is a certain vanity that I have about my appearance. I try to wear what I think looks good on me. I have a collection of scarves, *abayas*, and *dupattas* that no one is forcing me to put on every day and sometimes, I wonder, what if...?

But right now, all this is conjecture and supposition. It has still not stopped me from wearing the hijab...yet.

Loving a Headscarf
Scotty Enyart

> *"I hate quotations. Tell me what you know."*
> ~Ralph Waldo Emerson

I was a young college student just waking up to a world outside of the dominant, conservative, Christian worldview I was born into. Growing up in central California, ethnic diversity was never lacking in my life. Quite the opposite, in fact. My communities were in fact rich in ethnic diversity. Religious diversity, however, was another story. We may have looked different, but we all shared similar styles of dress, political views, and religious beliefs. It wasn't until college that I started to encounter and formulate deeper relationships with people from outside of the Christian world view I grew up in.

It was during an Intro to Psychology course that I met Nadine. On the first day of class our professor assigned the two of us to a group, and we would remain a team for the rest of the semester. Reflecting back on the situation twelve years ago, my first interest in Nadine was more of curiosity as to why she wore the hijab. I didn't think we could actually have enough in common to sustain a friendship. The hijab was such a strong symbol to me that identified her as "overly religious," I felt like any individual personality that Nadine might have had was lost to her religious beliefs.

My assumption was that she was a prudish girl who would be open to discussing only a very narrow range of topics. My initial encounters with her were very formal. I was cautious in what I said to her because I thought she would be easily offended. Other than getting our assignments done I didn't pay her too much attention. When I did think about her it was thoughts such as, "I wonder if she combs her hair? I wonder if she has to sleep with that *thing* on? I wonder if she is forced to wear the scarf?" At the time I didn't know it was called a hijab so I referred to it as a "scarf" or a "thing."

But we were in a psychology class and, by definition, the class forced us to talk about topics at the core of what it means to be human. It was when I began to hear her talk freely about her thoughts on the world that she started to capture my attention and I began to see her unique personality. I found myself paying attention to her more often and not just when prompted by the professor. She was incredibly funny and would often pass me notes in class joking about the topics. I really enjoyed the topics we discussed in the class but gradually I grew more excited to attend the class to speak with Nadine than to engage in the topics.

I once caught her doodling in class. She was drawing a picture of an eye, and so I did what every young psychology student does and over analyzed this to somehow mean she may be feeling oppressed because she has to wear the hijab. I imagined that she felt trapped and unable to express herself and only through the eyes could she communicate her deep feelings of oppression. Drawing an eye was a way of looking through the window of the eye to remember the creative person deep inside. I could not contemplate how wearing a hijab could be anything but oppression. The only way I could begin to understand why someone would wear a hijab was that they held archaic religious beliefs that were out of date in our current expressive society. I assumed that she felt she would be punished by God or her community if she chose not to wear the hijab. By now we had a good rapport and I didn't feel that I had to be so formal around her, and so I asked her how she felt about wearing the hijab (by now I was calling it by its proper name).

To me the thing that most strongly identified her physical appearance was the thing I felt I had to avoid talking about. I guess it was my idea that the hijab was oppressive that made me feel it was also taboo. Nadine happily responded to my question. Surprisingly, she really enjoyed talking about the hijab. I felt that our friendship deepened when I asked her about it. Her response was foreign to my Western views and I realized it was her choice because she wanted people to appreciate her for her intellect and not her looks. I explained my theory about her feeling oppressed and drawing the eye, and that got a big laugh out of her. Her response was, "I don't know why I drew the eye. I like drawing eyes." I felt a little embarrassed by my comments, as if I had completely misunderstood her and put her in a small box without really knowing her. But she eased my pain by laughing it off.

Gradually we carried the topics in class over into walks to the library. Our walks got longer and longer. I looked forward to walking with her and talking about life, differences, and similarities. These walks turned into three hour talks. We went on to coordinate our class schedules for the next couple of semesters and became close study partners. We would often plan to meet at the school on the weekends to study together. I think it was more to find a reason to meet and less to do with needing to study.

One day I asked her questions about her hair. "What color is your hair? Is it curly? What would happen if I saw your hair?" Nadine answered all of my questions candidly and then, the following week, she brought a picture album of her cousin's wedding. As I was flipping through the pictures she pointed to a picture of herself without the hijab on. I had a hard time recognizing her with hair. I felt warm and happy having her show me pictures with her hijab off. But, at the same time, I was also uncomfortable and didn't know how to respond to it. My first thought was to tell her how beautiful her hair was, but I didn't. I knew I wasn't supposed to be seeing that picture, according to her beliefs. Early in our friendship I would come up from behind her and tap her on the shoulder to get her attention. She made it clear to me that it wasn't appropriate for me to touch her and she also went on to talk about how it would not be appropriate for a man to see her hair unless it is her husband.

It was clear to me that her motivation for showing me her cousin's wedding pictures was for me to see her without the hijab on. She wanted me to see her without any barriers. I knew that we were starting to have feelings for each other that were more than just friendship. But it was still very difficult to comprehend how much we had started liking each other. She made it clear to me that her mother and father were traditional Muslims from Pakistan and would not accept her dating outside of her religion. It was these rigid categories of who you can date and who you can't date that made me — us — blind to the deeper emotional connection that was happening between us.

One day, for my birthday, Nadine gave me a journal so that I had something to write my thoughts in. It was a special gift that I continue to use even now. On the front of the journal she taped the picture of the eye she drew in class. She had held on to it! I smile widely even now, thinking about this. I'm reminded of her humour. I took the journal and wrote some ideas in it and then a week later I asked her to read what I had written. When I got it back she had added to the journal with her thoughts. We continued to pass the journal back and forth, adding a couple of pages each time. They were innocent love notes, exploring the early stages of a relationship that we could not express physically.

The back and forth with the journal was emotionally energizing. The writings were alluding to a relationship between us but in the third person. I vividly recall one of her writings, in which a woman was getting ready for bed, combing her hair, pondering her stressful day. The details in her writings were full of smell and touch and sight, about a physical connection with her. It was at this time that it hit me that I had fallen for her. The only thing that I looked forward to during this time was to see her. As a psychologist, I look back at this relationship and am fascinated by the dynamics of the connection. But at the time, it was not an intellectual exercise but rather a visceral bond. When I would think about her I would picture her without the hijab on, like I saw in the picture she showed me. To this date I have never been so infatuated by thoughts of a woman's hair. This was different than any attraction I have ever experienced.

I didn't have an image of her body — only her face and her hair held me to her physical appearance. The emphasis of my attraction to her was on her humour, intelligence, and kindness — her hair was really the only thing that kept me in the physical realm. As a man raised with a Western perspective, you learn to talk about certain parts of woman's body that you are most attracted to. In the most inner circles of "guy talk" we are pressured to choose what we are most attracted to about a woman: are you a breast man, a leg man, hips, the list goes on. As the writing became more intense I realized that my psyche was more stimulated than my physical self.

This relationship had happened so slowly and naturally that I found myself in love with her, never even realizing it was happening. Something happened in both of us. I know she felt the same toward me and it was as if, when we became conscious of liking each other, things started to become distant. We walked together less. It seemed as if we always had something to do after class and didn't have time to talk. We both knew our worlds were very different. I knew I'd never become Muslim and she didn't want to live a life separated from her faith, her family's belief system. There were times when I thought about converting to her belief system just to be able to be with her but I knew that was not the life that I wanted to live.

The last day of my undergrad programme we took a walk and indirectly told each other how we felt. We made plans to see each other over the summer. But those plans were a fairy tale. The very next day I received a long email from her. It was a nice email but in it she confessed that our relationship had made her think about and do things that took her away from her faith. She felt guilty about showing me pictures of her hair and the writings we shared with each other. Her words and her internal struggle between love and faith, in turn, made me feel guilty. I had done this to her. We had done this to each other. She asked me to never contact her again because it would be best that way.

The email hurt, but, in my heart, I knew it was for the best. I swallowed my feelings and thanked her for her honesty. And I promised to stay away. Perhaps at another point in my life, I wouldn't have given up so easily. But life is about timing, and that stage of my life was over. I graduated and was soon flying out to live in Asia for a study abroad programme. I was sad to see my relationship with Nadine end, but the excitement of the next stage of my life was already pulling me forward. That's not to say that I haven't thought about her over the years. I have. But I've never regretted our decision to part ways. The hijab is what attracted me to her but it was also what pushed us apart.

That was our last contact, twelve years ago. It was a different kind of attachment than I've ever had before. Even though I fell in love with her mind, it was the thought of running my fingers through her hair that has stayed with me all these years.

High School Hijabi
Yvonne Pilar Mesa El Ashmawi

> *"The struggle has always been inner,*
> *and is played out in the outer terrains."*
> ~Gloria Anzaldua, *Borderlands/La Frontera: The New Mestiza*

One Saturday afternoon during a trip to the mall, my mother asked me why I covered my hair from Muslim men who potentially wanted to marry me, but didn't cover in front of the boys at school who weren't interested in me. And that is how I was guilted into wearing hijab to school.

The following Friday I found myself in my high school counsellor's office. She looked up and asked me why I had scheduled a meeting with her. I couldn't tell her that it was my mother, of course, who made me talk to her. My mother had insisted that I alert the school. I suppose it did not occur to her that she could have — or perhaps should have — gone with me to facilitate that conversation. Instead, I told the counsellor that I stopped by her office to tell her that on Monday I would be coming to school wearing hijab, the Muslim woman's head-covering.

Our conversation was brief. She didn't ask me why I decided to wear. In retrospect, that was probably a good thing because I couldn't have even begun to explain the layers of reasons for my sudden decision. Only one or two of those reasons had anything to do with religion.

When I got on the bus Monday morning, the only other Muslim on the bus – a cute boy I had a crush on named Ahmed – pretended that he didn't know me, that we didn't attend the same mosque. The rest of the students on the bus took turns gawking and whispering, whispering and gawking.

When I was a teenager in California, I didn't know any other Muslim girls who wore the hijab to public school. My little circle of Muslim Youth Group friends consisted of less than ten girls. Only four of us even attended a public school; the rest were homeschooled. Of the four of us who made the daily bus trip to our local high school, I was the only one who wore hijab. We were scattered across the city and none of my friends went to my school. I felt so isolated. The homeschooled girls didn't understand the challenges I faced even though they wore hijab. Wearing it to the grocery store was not at all the same as wearing it every day down the hallways of my high school, facing the judgment of people I wanted to impress more than I wanted to be alive. The other three girls in public schools had nice moms who never expected them to wear it to school. I envied them their ability to fit in.

To my surprise, things settled down easily enough. After the first week or so of questions, the kids in my small school stopped staring and stopped asking. My friends asked why I didn't tell them before I started wearing it. I didn't know what to say, but the truth is that I just assumed that once they saw me in it, they wouldn't want to be my friends anymore. I imagined them pretending that they didn't know me and had never been friends with me. I imagined them (and not Ahmed) being like Ahmed. Instead, they told me that I was the same girl I was before I wore it and then we put the whole issue away until late May, when the first copies of the yearbook came out sprinkled with pictures of me with my beautiful, brown, waist-length hair. There were pictures of me and my hair at the Future Business Leaders of America conference, on the soccer field, in the cafeteria, at the Walk-a-thon; each picture was a reminder of the brown locks I now took great measures to hide. Yearbook pictures, after all, are always taken in the first semester, and I had started wearing hijab in February. My friends and I never talked about it, but I saw them look back and forth from the pictures to me when they thought I wasn't looking.

Wearing it to school was actually the final step to becoming a full-time hijabi. I don't remember a part of my childhood in which I didn't wear hijab at least part of the time. When I was younger than nine I wore it to the mosque and sometimes when we visited friends. When I was nine, I wore it everywhere except school. At least that is how I remember it. This may not be the case, but I do know I wore it the overwhelming majority of the time when I wasn't in school. And the thing is, I liked wearing it. My mother bought lots of scarves, so there were always a variety of colours available. There were also multiple white scarves and black scarves, each with different designs. My mother used to put them in a scarf drawer as fair game for either of us to use, something I would later do with my own girls.

When I became a woman (Is this not the most old school way to describe puberty?) and my mother's friend gave me the talk, I went through a kind of golden age of clothing. I had beautiful scarves and began finding my own aesthetic, of which I still see traces in the style in which I dress now. I loved fitted tops and dresses and fit-and-flare skirts in beautiful, rich colours. When I looked in the mirror I saw someone I began to think may have some beauty after all. Of course, this impression was quickly shattered by a few offhand critiques. But sometimes, like when I wore my white fitted top with turquoise colored flowers and a long fit-and-flare turquoise skirt, I looked in the mirror and thought, "This girl could have potential." Like the stirrings I sometimes felt when I was alone, I hid the thought that I could be beautiful from everyone, usually even me.

The first comment I remember as a hijabi was in high school when I was a senior. I had moved from my home town to Phoenix, Arizona. I had already endured the stares through all of eleventh grade, when one day in the twelfth grade, a boy I had a crush on told me that the fact that I covered my hair made him wonder what I looked like under all of the clothes. I was young enough and naïve enough to take this as a compliment. It would be decades later that I would connect this to the ways in which Muslim women who wear hijab are exoticized and fetishized, the headscarf and accompanying sartorial choices rendering Muslim women at once invisible and hypervisible in society.

The first devastating comments I remember also happened when I was a senior. One day I was walking across the quad and I ran into my favourite teacher. I was wearing a green dress and a white scarf. I know that doesn't sound like it matches, but in those days the white scarf was the trend, white scarves supposedly going with everything. We exchanged hellos and I was happy walking with her as I was on my way to her class. She looked at me, with her grey blonde hair and blue eyes behind the Sally Jesse Rafael glasses and said, "Your scarf makes you look so messy; you'll never be able to get a job with that on your head."

I felt like she had punched me in the stomach. I was so embarrassed. She called me messy. Did I always look messy? I wore a white scarf every day, except when I wore black, the other fashionable colour. Did I always look ugly? We walked the rest of the way to class in an awkward silence. We never had a personal conversation after that.

She didn't make me stop wearing it, but not too long after that incident, which had blind-sided me because she was my favourite teacher, I stopped wearing it to school. It wasn't her fault that the rest of my high school years turned into an on-again off-again romance with the hijab. I wanted boys to think I was attractive and I felt that they never did because I was in hijab. Instead, I began wearing eyeliner, t-shirts and shorts to school, and then before driving myself home I would change back into my modest jeans and scarf and wipe off whatever was left of the eyeliner.

I wanted to fit in so badly I could taste it. It stayed with me night and day. I had so many other reasons to be self-conscious. I was already a size 18 — little did I know that was only the beginning of my climbing dress size — and I was the only brown person that went to my school. There were other Mexicans at my school, but in the honours classes I had fought to get into, I was the only person of color in a sea of white faces. My white friends were bussed in from the better neighborhoods, so they always talked in terms of how they were the victims of reverse racism and how they were doing the school a favour, making it better, by coming here instead of their *real* school. I felt I was ugly and I so wanted to be beautiful.

I thought if I took off my scarf, boys would notice me. So I took my scarf off. Male teachers noticed me, staring me up and down, one even putting his arm around me and telling me how absolutely stunning I looked. Again, I was naïve enough to think that a teacher's sexual attentions could be a compliment. However, no one in my honours clique noticed. Instead, they blinked at me for a second and then got on with their lives. It hit me and crushed me that I was just an ugly girl, like my step-father used to tell me; the scarf had nothing to do with anything. It was something inside me that kept men at a distance, something in my essence. I was ugly down to the marrow of my bones. I was ugly at the very cellular level.

But there was one guy who thought I wasn't ugly. He had told me he was attracted to me because I was the only girl who could give him a run for his money in honours history. My honours clique invited me to a party one night and I dressed up for the first time ever in a miniskirt. It was red and I wore a fitted white blouse and a black belt and low heels. My crush's father had passed away not too long before, and so when I got there he was sitting alone in the living room.

We played typical party games, including a game in which a guy chose a girl in the room and stared deep into her eyes and said, "I love you baby, but I just can't smile," and then the girl would have to say it back without smiling. He said it to me. I trembled and melted inside, but I returned his gaze and very firmly, very seriously said, "I love you, baby, but I just can't smile." He repeated it twice more and then said, "I give up! She won't smile."

This, of course, made me smile.

He asked me later that evening to go with him for a ride on his motorcycle and he kissed me under the moonlight. I knew that all of it — the party, the *I love you*, the motorcycle ride, and the midnight kiss — would never have happened with hijab.

Where I Least Expected to Meet a Woman in Hijab
Kathryn Kraft

> *"A woman of valour who can find? For her price is far above rubies...*
> *Strength and dignity are her clothing."*
> ~Book of Proverbs, Chapter 31

She walked into the little meeting room, which was separated from the church sanctuary by a window. On Sundays, mothers of small children used the room to look after their little ones while following along with the songs and preaching happening in the adjacent hall. But on weekdays, dark red velvet curtains were pulled shut over the window. Two sofas filled the room, making it a comfortable space for both meetings and casual conversations. By the time the woman joined us, I had been in the room for two hours already, interviewing a series of different church members about their relationship to the community around them. The church was located in a Lebanese town which had both Christian and Muslim residents, and I was enjoying the series of stories about how church volunteers interacted with their diverse array of neighbours.

I'd seen her walking around the halls, so I wasn't surprised when she walked in. In fact, I was glad finally to be formally introduced to this cheery church worker who had already caught my eye. Slight in stature, she looked confident and efficient as she went about her business, with her head covered in proper Muslim fashion. Her hijab, indeed her entire outfit, was stylish, colourful and flattering. But still, I was struck by a bout of cognitive dissonance — a Christian church employee dressed distinctively as a Muslim was not a typical sight.

Her colleague, a long-time church member whom I had just finished interviewing, excused himself to find some cups, hot water and packets of Nescafé. The woman sat down next to me, perched delicately on the sofa, hands in her lap, and listened as I introduced myself. I began asking her my pre-set list of interview questions and she graciously answered each one with a concise and thoughtful answer. Soon, our host returned with the coffee and sat down on the broad couch across from us. As we stirred our drinks, he told me that I should — no — I *must* hear her conversion story. With pride, he told me that she was one of the church's newest members, and her story was beautiful.

Awkwardly, I obliged, and asked her if she would be willing to share. This was not the reason for which I had asked to meet her and I was trying very hard not to make a big deal of the fact that her dress indicated, so boldly, that she was a Muslim, and yet she worked and worshipped in a church. She didn't seem to mind, though, and began telling me about her spiritual journey. Clearly this was not the first time she'd been called upon to share what church members would call "her testimony".

She explained that she was not really into religion before she came to this town, to which she had moved a few years before in order to be closer to her husband's family. Adjusting to life had been difficult for her. Her sister-in-law was from the Shi'a branch of Islam, but she herself was Sunni Muslim. Living with her in-laws, she was exposed for the first time to Shi'a teachings, which were a fair bit different from what she had been raised to believe. Then some members of the Ahbash movement came for a visit. The Ahbash are Sufi mystics who blend Shi'a and Sunni teachings and engage in charitable work in poor Muslim communities. They started talking to her about their beliefs, leaving her even more confused. Eventually, one of the church volunteers chanced upon her. He came to bring her family charitable aid. But when he started talking with her about his Christian faith, she was left even more overwhelmed. Everyone was teaching her something different!

Because her family was in a very difficult situation financially, she visited the church, hoping to learn more about the assistance they had to offer. On this visit, the church volunteers invited her to attend a food distribution, a short church meeting after which she would receive enough staples to feed her family for the better part of the next month. She told me that she was overwhelmed by the kindness of the people she met at the church.

"I saw a different love," she explained. "I wondered, why do they work with us in this way?" Since moving to this town, she had felt neglected or mistreated by almost everyone she had met. "When you just enter the church, though, it's different. I learned that it's because of Christ. They care about all aspects of our life."

One of the things the preacher said at the distribution meeting was that prayer had power. She was unemployed at the time and had been looking for a job without results, so she decided to test the statement about prayer. She prayed to God that, if she found a job, she would pay more attention to Him. And within a week she was offered a job! She told me a few other stories of little things that happened that kept reaffirming her interest in a spiritual world, and most of these little things pointed her attention towards the church. So after only a few months in her new town, she said, "God entered my heart."

The church members who had become her friends were ecstatic that she had committed herself to their faith. It wasn't long after this that they caught on to the fact that she had some strong professional skills that were being underutilized in her current job. So, the church offered her a paid position.

At this point in the conversation, I couldn't pretend not to notice anymore. She had just shared her heart, and told of a highly controversial, highly sensitive religious conversion about which she would probably not even be able to tell her family. And she had told it in such a simple, unassuming way. In my many years in the Middle East, I had grown accustomed to interfaith coexistence, usually peaceful and friendly, but occasionally horridly contentious. I had several friends who were married across faith lines. I knew Muslims who celebrated Christmas and Christians who celebrated Eid. I had even met a number of people who were converts from one faith tradition to another.

But there were some lines that were not to be crossed.

One of those lines was that of a woman's dress. A woman would never worship in a mosque with her head uncovered, nor would a woman ever wear hijab in church. Traditional Christian women might cover their heads in a church service, but their head covering was easily distinguished from the hijab. For example, a Christian woman might wear an embroidered lace doily that barely covered a few square inches of hair; it would not look, even remotely, Muslim. Greek Orthodox nuns would cover themselves more thoroughly, but they lived together as members of a religious order so they, too, would not likely be mistaken for Muslim.

In the past few years, though, when visiting churches in the Middle East, I had begun to notice a handful of women in worship services wearing hijab. From the dress, an astute observer would know not only her religion, but the particulars of her religious sect and possibly even her home village. They would definitely know that a woman dressed in this manner was not from a Christian family and thus did not belong in church! Somehow, this line-that-was-never-to-be-crossed had been fading away. So, in all honesty, I was pleased to meet this young woman who not only attended church wearing hijab, but had taken on employment and joined the church's ministry team — unapologetically dressed as a Muslim. Perhaps she could help explain this phenomenon.

"Please forgive me," I started. "I have met converts from Islam to Christianity before, but I have never met a woman who still wears hijab in church. How do people treat you? Why do you do it?"

"I have been treated very well," she replied readily. "I don't feel strange."

I nodded, signaling her to continue.

"Well," she went on, "You could say there are two types of people in the church. There are those who are not, say, full believers. They do treat me oddly, and seem to be scared. The full believers, no, they welcome me. Maybe they do pay a bit extra attention because of it, but I see the way I dress as a message. It tells of who I was, who I am and who I have become."

I understood her to be saying that Christians who did not accept a sister worshipper dressed like her were not true Christians at all. She continued to dress as she always had, in order to honour her family and her hometown and her culture. And, as far as she was concerned, her clothing had nothing to do with her faith.

But it certainly did draw attention.

In all my attempts to be nonchalant, even I had asked her about her outfit. I had many close friends who dressed like her, so her clothing looked normal to me. It just looked a bit out of place in a church, so I could certainly imagine how much more shocking her appearance might be to a church member who had hardly travelled and who had few friends outside the Christian community. Although people in her own church were growing used to her presence with them, others — even church leaders — were not always sure how to respond.

She told me about a time when she visited a church in another town. Upon meeting her, the leader of that church asked, "Does your pastor dress you this way?" He said it in a jovial tone, but she could tell from the look in his eyes that he was not teasing. It was an accusation against her and against her pastor.

Speaking to her, I was struck by the confidence with which she spoke about the incident. She knew who she was and who she wanted to be, which she expressed through her actions and in her friendships with other members of the church. She loved her heritage and her family, and saw no reason to reject that, but she also loved the new faith and relationships she had found in the church.

"At first I was hurt," she shared. "It was hard to hear. But then I realized the problem was his."

Ghūṅghaṭa: A Patriarchal Tool for Veiling Women's Subjectivity and Sexuality

Sukhdev Singh and Satwant Kaur

> *"Woman is never anything but the locus of a more or less competitive exchange between two men."*
> ~Luce Irigaray

The following essay is based on conversations with Satwant Kaur. It is her voice that I hope to convey.

***

Before marriage I was called Kuntī. Kuntī is a prominent female character in the *Mahābhārata*, an epic narrative about the Kurukshetra War. It is considered one of the longest poems in history — nearly ten times the length of Homer's classics, the *Odyssey* and the *Iliad,* combined — and its importance is often compared to the Bible or the Quran. In the story, Kuntī was kind to a sage named Durvāsā. In return, she was given a boon from him that she would be able to call upon any of the gods and bear a child. In the epic, she called upon Sūrya, or the sun god, who bore her a son. Afraid of being an unwed mother, she left the baby in a basket to float in the current of a nearby river.

But Kuntī was only one of the names by which I was known in my village. It is quite common in a rural Indian setting for names to be changed and corrupted, and so I was also called Kāntā or Kuntā. Another name that was used to address me was Śakuntalā. This name represented two very different characters. In the *Mahābhārata*, Śakuntalā was an outspoken and assertive woman and the mother of Bharata, after whom India is named. The other reference is in Kālīdasā's play, *Abhijñāna-śakuntalam*, or the Recognition of Śakuntalā. In the play, Śakuntalā was a submissive woman, helpless under the patriarchal society she inhabited. All these names were changed after my marriage in 1981. My husband named me Āshā, which in English means hope, but because of my father-in-law's dominance as the patriarch of the house, it was never allowed to become my official name. Instead, my father-in-law named me Satwant Kaur, which has been my official name ever since. All of these names are valid and continue to be used to address me in different contexts.

I was born in a small village in Haryana, an Indian state that forms the northern, western and southern borders of Delhi, the capital of India. The state of Haryana, in which my village is located, is infamous for its disproportionate ratio of males to females, resulting from the rampant practice of female foeticide, and the *khap* village councils that are against the inter-caste marriages of today's Indian youth. Because of some confusion, I have been told of two dates of my birth: 13 August 1959 and 15 August 1960. The latter is my official date of birth, but no one knows for certain which date is the accurate one. Such uncertainties are an integral part of the rural Indian populace as everyday life is not bound by written rules. In fact, rural Indian life exists orally in its entirety. Rules of conduct and the laws that govern behaviour are generally not written, but transferred orally from one generation to the next. This is done by inducting each generation into the practice. I belong to that generation in the past for which learning took place by following the rituals that were practised by elders. *Ghūṅghaṭa* was one such practice.

My focus here is on the Hindu and Sikh traditions, so in discussing this topic, I refer to women of these two religions only. The *ghūṅghaṭa* is a veil that is used to cover the heads and often the faces of married Indian women. This veil can be made from the end of a sari or from a long sheer scarf known as a *dupaṭṭa*. The *dupaṭṭa* serves as an accessory to the *salawara-kamiza*, which consists of a tunic and pantaloons. A *dupaṭṭa*-turned-*ghūṅghaṭa* is of many types. In many rural communities of my time, only the eyes were left naked; while in others, it was just the head that remained covered. Often, the *dupaṭṭa*-turned-*ghūṅghaṭa* was wrapped around the head and neck, with the ends falling in layers across a woman's chest or down her back.

Like many habits that one absorbs while growing up, young Indian girls of my generation developed an awareness of, and many a times fascination for, the practise of the *ghūṅghaṭa* by watching others follow it in their families. And so, I learned about the *ghūṅghaṭa*, by seeing my sister-in-law practice it. I also learned about it by watching other married women in my village. Its relevance was not inside books or within the walls of a school building, but rather in the behaviours of the married women around me. Although a restrictive garment, which created difficulty in physical movement, the *ghūṅghaṭa* symbolized the essence of a woman. What it meant then and even now is *lāja* or *śarma*. Both terms are translated as shame, but are generally used to convey the sense of shyness which is expected and, indeed, revered in an Indian woman.

By connecting the *ghūṅghaṭa* with the essential qualities of "a good woman", the practice became an inextricable part of our virtue. To maintain this virtue, then, a married woman adopted the *ghūṅghaṭa* in front of the male elders on her husband's side. This included the father-in-law, the elder brother of the husband, and all the elders in the community. It was not a requirement in one's maternal home, which reflects the two interrelated dimensions of the *ghūṅghaṭa* that are rarely acknowledged – shame and sexuality. The absence of the *ghūṅghaṭa* was notable in decimating the honour of a married woman within the confines of her husband's family and community.

A *dupaṭṭa*-turned-*ghūṅghaṭa*
© Baljeet Singh, reproduced by permission

It should be noted that the *ghūṅghaṭa* was and continues to be exclusively prescribed for women, not for men. Patriarchy is a global phenomenon across cultures, religions and nations. The whole world is united and organized under the aegis of male dominance. Women who are subjected to patriarchal norms are forced to either hide from view or have our own vision obstructed in some way.

165

Imagine a photograph of a person, be it a female or a male, whose head and face have been scraped off or smudged. Would you be able to identify this person? Most probably, not! As identification — the ability to be recognized in the crowd – is the key to individuality, our personhood is ultimately determined by our face and head. A headless body does not readily provide one's identity. By covering those parts that provide us with an identity, we are successfully degraded as a human being into just a mere collection of body parts.

In patriarchal structures, a woman's personhood and her sexuality are inextricably linked. It is not just her face or her head, but her entire body that is considered to be sexual. If a woman's personhood is a matter of shame as the cultural practise of the *ghūṅghaṭa* implies, it must be hidden away. By linking shame with honour, the *ghuṅghaṭa* becomes an efficient tool to do away with a woman's agency and render her invisible. In a patriarchal culture, such as my village in Haryana, a woman is considered to be a transactional commodity. She is owned like a product and may be exchanged from one man to another. Her sexuality is like a prize to be won by competing men. Once married, the owner of a woman's personhood and sexuality is primarily her husband. But as her owner, he can swap her to another man, including a family member, if he so desires or is pressured to do so. From this perspective, the wife needs to remain covered from the view of her father-in-law, her husband's elder brother, and any older males in the family as these are by default fellow competitors. Thus, the *ghūṅghaṭa* is not only an opaque screen behind which a married woman's personhood is hidden. It is also a stamp, branding or sign that she is owned by someone.

When I was growing up, only elderly women were exempt from the confines of the veil. Perhaps old age was considered immune to or free from shame. More likely, a woman's sexuality – her prize – was considered less desirable by men as she aged. If a young married woman did not adopt the *ghūṅghaṭa*, she was called shameless and without manners. She would certainly be chastised by the society around her. It is quite possible that today a married woman in my village might not have to undergo the same experiences as the married women of my time, but I cannot say that with certainty. Women are still not considered equal to men. We are akin to men's footwear — changeable at any time.

I became free from the veil, but it came with a price.

There was an immense feud in the family and I was forced to grapple with my father-in-law. I did not realize what it meant then, but it was a point from which there was no turning back. I will not go into the details here, but the consequences of those events changed everything. The feud took away my husband's life. After that, I adopted the *ghūṅghaṭa* in front of neither my father-in-law nor anyone else. Freedom can be a painful experience; one cannot get free with ease. I know this because I paid dearly for my freedom.

Perhaps this generation is far more sagacious and pragmatic than we were. If I were to offer any wisdom to the women of this generation, it would be this: Do not practice the *ghūṅghaṭa*. I do not wish for you to bear the weight of such exploitative cultural practices. In our country, the *ghūṅghaṭa* is a visual representation of the inequality between men and women. I think if such elements did not exist, women might have a chance to be seen as equal to men.

And also perhaps, to be free like them.

PART 4

A LESSER MUSLIM?

Never Good Enough
Shaheen Pasha

"We have to confront ourselves. Do we like what we see in the mirror?
And, according to our light, according to our understanding, according to
our courage, we will have to say yea or nay – and rise!"
~Maya Angelou

The phone calls would start as soon as I entered my house. I knew they were coming and I was desperate to avoid them. Climbing down from the school bus, I would make multiple stops on the short walk to my family's town house – the last house on our *cul-de-sac* – looking for any distraction along the way to delay my journey home.

But it was never long enough. As soon as I opened the door and pulled off my jacket, the incessant ringing would begin. Sighing, I would put down my book bag and walk over to the phone hanging from the wall.

"Assalamu'Alaykum, sister. I need to speak to you about your hair," said the soft voice on the other end.

I've never figured out what the big deal is surrounding my hair. As far as hair goes, I have always considered mine to be fairly ordinary: straight and dark brown, hardly anything worth fussing about. But for as long as I can remember, my hair has always been both a source of interest and consternation for the people in my life. When I was a young child, I loved to let it flow free, snarled and uncombed. It suited my wild spirit but annoyed my mother, who eventually cut it into a short bob in the middle of the night, while I slept. I woke up in the morning, my head feeling light and my neck tingling from the cold.

"It was driving me crazy," my mother said when I looked at myself in the mirror in horror. "If you can't take care of it, you can't have long hair." That was my first lesson in the power of my hair.

As I grew older, I opted to keep the short hair. I was a tomboy by nature and a boy cut helped me assimilate with the group of boys I played tag with in elementary school. Without my long hair, I didn't feel the need to wear dresses or play with girlie toys. My roughhousing and tomboy ways stayed with me until I was about to enter junior high school. Suddenly my hair became a problem once again. I was sitting at a dinner party, when an auntie came up to me, as

Pakistani aunties are wont to do.

"Are you a boy? Why do you have such short hair? You're getting too old to look like a boy. Listen to my advice, grow your hair out or you're going to have a problem as you grow up. Boys don't want to marry a girl that looks like a boy." With that, she walked away to get another soda. I sat there looking at my plate, my appetite gone.

I tried not to admit it, but her words stayed with me. I was entering middle school and starting to like boys. What if she was right? I slowly began to grow my hair out. It reached my shoulders, it reached my waist, and eventually it fell in a thick, dark mass to nearly my knees. My mother became possessive of it and paranoid that someone would put the evil eye on me for having such long, beautiful hair. I was not allowed to leave it loose and trimming my hair became a battle, with only my older sister allowed to take a pair of scissors to it. I was suffocated by my hair but empowered at the same time. My hair became my one symbol of beauty at a time when I felt like an awkward adolescent. And when a boy I liked came up behind me in high school, pulled my hair tie out and whispered that he loved my hair loose, I remember getting butterflies.

And then the phone calls started.

I was living in Central New Jersey at the time, a senior at a high school that seemed to be going through some sort of religious revival. The Muslim students I had laughed and joked with just one year earlier were now becoming more outwardly religious. The boys began growing beards and wearing long kurtas over their jeans. And the girls were suddenly covering their hair and taking it upon themselves to enlighten other Muslim sisters in the school to do the same. I was one of their projects.

Putting hijab on my hair became the personal mission of one Muslim sister, in particular. Her name was Yasmeen and she was a convert. She had not only donned the hijab but had also taken to covering her face and wearing a full burka to school. There was no doubt she was serious about her beliefs. And I, with my long hair now worn loose at school in rebellion at my mom's strict admonitions, was an affront to her.

So she began to call me. Every day.

And in her soft voice, she would lecture me about being a good Muslim. Did I not love God? If I did, how could I take the beauty He had given me and parade it around other men? Did I not realize that every time I walked past men with my hair uncovered, I was disrespecting the other Muslim women? That I was acting as if I was above them and trying to tempt the other Muslim brothers?

"If you were to ever to bother to pray salat, you would know that it's required to cover your hair when you stand before God," she argued one afternoon. I jumped on this as the one thing I had a tangible argument for.

"I do pray," I told her. I was not a bad Muslim, I reasoned.

She simply sighed and said, "Sister, do you think God will accept the prayers of someone who only covers her hair in front of Him but immediately goes back to waving her hair in front of men, seducing them, as soon as she steps off the prayer mat?"

The words struck me like a smack in the face. I considered myself to be religious. I prayed five times a day. I wore loose, baggy clothes that hid my figure and I refused to date, putting off would-be boyfriends with the explanation that it was against my religion to be with a man before marriage. I tried to be a good person to my friends and a good daughter to my parents, believing that I was a good Muslim. But after I hung up the phone on Yasmeen that afternoon, all I could think was that I just wasn't good enough. At the end of the day, it didn't matter what I did. My worth as a Muslim would be measured only by the piece of cloth that I chose not to wrap around my head.

I refused to admit it for years, but Yasmeen's words poisoned something inside of me. I developed a very complex relationship with hijab through college and my twenties. Before, I had seen all Muslim women as the same. We were all sisters on different places on the same spectrum. I didn't judge a hijabi and I didn't feel judged by one. But that all changed in the aftermath of those phone calls. Suddenly, as more Muslim girls I knew began to don the hijab, I felt isolated. I felt judged. I felt like there was a club that I no longer belonged to. I could observe it but always as a woman on the periphery. Over time, I stopped caring about belonging to that Muslim club. I did my own thing, practised religion my own way and vowed that I would only marry a man who was open to loving me the way I was.

And I eventually did. My husband comes from a very conservative family. The mosque is their second home. Vacations are taken in Saudi Arabia where they can go to *Umrah* and women go to religious education classes and compare hijab styles. But my husband was different. He didn't expect or want me to cover my hair if that was something I didn't want to do. He told me that he loved my hair loose the way it was. He loved me the way I was.

Unfortunately, his family didn't feel the same. On my first trip to visit them after my marriage, I was excitedly getting dressed in an elaborate Indian lengha, befitting a new bride. My make up was perfect, my hair was styled in a perfect chignon. I felt beautiful. As I prepared to walk down to meet some of my husband's extended family, my mother-in-law stopped me.

"You look nice," she said, taking in my appearance. "Just put this on and then you can go down and I'll introduce you to everyone." She pulled out a white hijab and promptly tied it around my hair. "Now, you're good," she said and walked away.

I felt small. After everything, I still wasn't good enough. I still needed to put a piece of cloth on my head in order to gain approval, this time from members of my husband's family.

I walked into the bathroom where my husband was combing his hair. He took one look at me and called his mom in.

"Don't ask her to wear that again," he said, pulling the hijab off my head. "She is perfect the way she is and if anyone doesn't like it, then there is something wrong with them."

With that one declaration from my husband, the poison that I had been ignoring in my heart began to dissipate. I didn't feel that my uncovered hair made me any less of a Muslim. I didn't feel like I wasn't good enough.

So now when a hijabi sister asks me if I have ever considered covering my hair, I don't hesitate to answer no. And when they inevitably say, "Maybe one day, *inshaAllah*," I have no qualms in responding with a smile:

"It's not for me. I'm good enough the way I am."

Seeking Cover
Zehra Naqvi

"When I see you through my eyes, I think that we are different.
When I see you through my heart, I know we are the same."
~Doe Zantamata

Like most modern relationships, my relationship with hijab is complicated. First, I'm not entirely sure where I fall on the spectrum of what constitutes hijab, whether it's just a head covering or an overall modest way of dressing. A lot of what I understand about hijab is informed by my background. I am a South Asian, Muslim-American immigrant female. There's a lot of contradiction within that smorgasbord of identities and managing the interaction between them has always been a delicate and confusing balancing act. Growing up, my background informed my everyday decisions on what clothes to wear, how to behave at home, and how to behave at school.

For most people around me, hijab generally refers to the loose-fitting clothing from head to toe, topped off with a headscarf. But the headscarf signifies different things to me depending on which identity lens I examine it through. In the South Asian culture, I generally saw head coverings confined to religious spaces and gatherings. In the Muslim context, the headscarf seemed to be a daily identifier, marking the female wearing it as Muslim. In the American context, it was something very different from the norm – a freak flag. Since my mom and sister only wore the headscarf in religious spaces and gatherings, I assumed I would just follow suit. I never imagined the head covering would become a critical part of my character development and a means by which communities, even my own, could make me feel like an outsider.

The character development part started in junior high. At age twelve, I had braces, acne, and terrible taste in clothing. My junior high school was not exactly diverse. New York City public school zoning protocols landed me in likely the only predominantly white school in Queens, with very few immigrants or minorities. My understanding of American culture, based mostly on TV and cafeteria conversations, was that my experience as an American teenage girl was supposed to be all about make-up, boyfriends, and parties. I felt bewildered by all of it – the onslaught of changes, the strange rites of passage, and the pressure to belong. I started to feel I didn't belong and, more importantly, I didn't really *want* to belong. All the insecurities of the age inspired me to find a different way to cope. I sought cover to fend off the pressure, and find a different approach to growing up and figuring out who I wanted to be. I started turning to my other identities for an alternative.

Literal cover turned out to be my answer. I let my freak flag fly.

I wore the headscarf for the first time on the first day of seventh grade. I naïvely thought that no one would really care about my decision. I certainly never expected the bullying. It was before 9/11, and few people knew what the scarf represented or what a Muslim was, but it was still a world where "different" translated into nonconforming, unfamiliar, and bizarre. I had just painted a big old bull's-eye on my back.

There was a lot of bullying and it was ugly. Kids pulled on my scarf, shoved me in the stairwells, and generally made me aware of just how different I had marked myself as being. The South Asian/Muslim/immigrant components made me think I should just suffer through it. So day after day, I took the abuse and didn't complain. But inside, there was growing rage about how I was being pushed around when all I wanted was to be left alone. One day, one too many kids pushed me and it resulted in an epic confrontation.

A scrawny 13-year-old, with meticulously gelled hair, ultimately became the recipient of my pent-up rage. One day, as I exited the cafeteria, I heard laughter behind me. Suddenly, my scarf was yanked hard enough to make the ends of the covering pull on my throat and make me cough and stumble. I heard him say something snarky as he joined his laughing cronies. Tears formed in my eyes. As usual, I started to walk away.

A few steps later, however, I stopped. After months of humiliation, I simply couldn't take it anymore. I suddenly found the courage to finally stand up for myself. I turned around, walked against the human current flowing from the cafeteria, and found him with his friends. His friends sensed trouble and stopped laughing. He didn't. I pinned him to the wall with my arm across his shoulders, holding up his scrawny frame. His face was a perfect picture of shock. Shaking and crying, I looked him in the eyes and said: "Don't you ever touch me again."

He made the mistake of laughing at me, the awkward laughter of a teen unsure about what was happening or how he was supposed to react. He said: "Okay, okay, relax (laugh), I was just joking around!"

I leaned in closer and said: "Look at me. Do I look like I'm joking right now? If you touch me again, I'll fucking hurt you." And I let my arm fall away, leaving him stumbling to find his footing.

After that day, not a single kid ever bothered me again. I walked around with confidence, practically daring people to pick on me. I went on to wear the scarf for a total of five years. Each year, my hijab style evolved. It went from a loose piece of fabric over my head with its ends slung over my shoulders to a tightly pinned form that didn't let any hair show. I cared less and less about fitting in. Ironically that drew even more people to me, particularly in the diverse high school I later ended up in. As I grew up, I started questioning everything, including my faith. But the scarf marked me in appearance as an ambassador of Islam. It was odd that I was exploring my commitment to my faith while I was also serving as a walking ad for it.

So I decided I didn't want to wear the scarf anymore.

I felt like I had achieved what I had wanted from the experience. I felt empowered as a young woman, not limited or confined to a physical form, fearless and bold for having worn the scarf, and brave for overcoming the bullying. I had broken out of my shell, ridden out the bad days, and now was curious to see if I could recognize who I was independent of it.

Taking off the hijab was an eye-opening experience. It absolutely changed how people behaved towards me. Before I was identified first as a Muslim. Now I was foremost a woman. It changed the nature of people's interactions with me. I somehow became more approachable so that people took on more of an air of familiarity with me. But I also found myself having to work harder to be taken seriously, to be accorded the same respect I seemed to have while wearing the covering. There were a lot of unexpected pros and cons that often made me wonder about whether I would ever take on the headscarf again.

When 9/11 happened, I often wondered how my experience would have been different if the timing had been different. After that day, I watched a number of young Muslim women (and Sikh men) face a lot of harassment, within and outside of the community, for their choice to cover their hair. As much of the world around me started picking on people for being Muslim, the Muslim-American part of my identity started playing a more prominent role in my life.

I started defending the choice of women wearing scarves to bullies on the public transportation system. I felt a solidarity with women who wore the headscarf and was outraged when they were victimized or told to change their choice. I wanted those women to feel safe in their decision and I also wanted people to know that not all Muslim women look the same. We are women who wear the scarf and women who don't. The scarf, *abaya,* or *niqab* are not our identifying marks. Our beliefs are. I realized during that time that I was adamantly pro-choice on the issue of hijab and about most issues relating to faith. It wasn't my place to tell others how to be Muslim and I didn't take kindly to others instructing me on the same.

For me, faith was a process of self-discovery and it required a thoughtful and well-reasoned approach as to its practice. My choices should be in the service of my relationship with God, not borne out of any societal expectations. I had already had the experience of having to defend my choice concerning the head covering outside of the community. But in 2004, I found myself defending another choice concerning hijab *within* my faith-based community.

That year, I took on an organizing role with a Muslim conference being held in a major cosmopolitan city. I liked the idea of a safe space for Muslims to gather and talk about what they had in common, their concerns, and what work remained to be done in safeguarding our interests.

Even though I generally donned the headscarf in mosques, this event was taking place in a hotel. I knew many women in attendance would be wearing hijab but I felt it would be hypocritical for me to don the scarf in the hotel for the duration of the conference, knowing I would remove it as soon as I left the conference grounds. It felt disingenuous and disrespectful to the idea of hijab, as well as the women who wore the headscarf full time. I anticipated getting some very harsh critique for my decision from some of the religious figures who would be present. I expected some of the attendees to be offended as well. I discussed the decision with my family and ultimately decided that it was important for me to come as I was. I wanted to show that Muslim women are not a homogenous group. So I came in the attire I would wear at any other professional conference: a business suit.

During one general session, I sat with a non-Muslim friend whom I had invited as a guest speaker for another panel. The main speaker during that session saw me sitting in the front row of the ballroom, without a headscarf, in a room where most (if not all) of the women had headscarves on. Before a packed house of hundreds of people, she proceeded to say how women who did not wear the scarf would have to answer for that decision to God one day. She kept looking at me and talked about how she was one of the people who washed the bodies of the departed before burial and when it was a woman who did not cover, she prayed particularly hard for God to forgive the woman for her choice.

I sat there feeling stunned, humiliated, and bullied all over again, but this time in a setting that I thought was supposed to be a safe space for Muslims. My non-Muslim friend sat alongside me, horrified. Any positive impression I had ever made on her about Islam and the Muslim community I took great pride in identifying with, was now marred by what she was witnessing. What she saw was a friend that sought to positively contribute to her community and change the negative perception of Muslims being publicly shamed by another member of her very own community, during a conference with "unity and diversity" as its theme. Sometime later, she asked if she could submit a piece about it to a Washington newspaper. I begged her not to, worried that it would not help to have an "outsider" to the community critique it. She didn't understand or agree, but she honoured my request. Now, ten years later, I think the critique she intended is valid, warranted, and long overdue...but from an insider this time.

So here it goes. I won't enter the fray on the Islamic definition of hijab, whether it includes more than a headscarf or whether it is a general instruction to dress modestly. I don't think it's my place to comment on how others perceive hijab or practice hijab. I can only tell you that it saddens me greatly to see the very thing that allowed me the opportunity to evolve in so many ways relegated to a mere uniform. To me, wearing the headscarf felt empowering, liberating, and dignified. My decision to wear the hijab was not undertaken lightly or as a mere rite of passage. It was a bold choice, one I remain proud of.

The fact that there are posters in most mosques requiring women to observe "hijab", depicting a woman in a headscarf but no corresponding posters about any other practice (including men growing beards) is unbalanced and, quite frankly, bizarre. I'm not advocating for pro-beard posters. I believe that the concept of hijab is, at times, being used arbitrarily to impose additional restrictions on women. It sets up an excuse to shame them, and deny them access and credibility on the basis of a headscarf. Seeing women denied access to Muslim conferences, or ostracized or harassed in Muslim gatherings in mosques, community centres, and non-religious spaces such as hotels for not wearing the headscarf reminds me of the bullies I encountered years ago. They sought to punish people who did not conform to their societal expectations and make them feel unwelcome based solely on an article of clothing. It created a world of insiders and outsiders.

The female speaker at the conference had a microphone, an audience of hundreds, and the opportunity to make a positive, unifying impact on her listeners. Had she spoken about the underlying rationale for why she believes hijab is mandatory, the positive attributes about hijab the way she chose to observe it, or her positive experience with it, that would have been powerful. It may have even inspired more women to consider donning the headscarf. But her remarks left me feeling unwelcome, like an outsider, and a blight upon my community's honour. And because she was given a prime time slot in the conference program to make such remarks, it begged the question, is this the modern face of our community?

I'm not attacking the conference or the speaker. But my fear is that we, as a community, are allowing our faith – which is something that I have always thought of as beautiful, inclusive, comforting, and welcoming – to become exclusive and limited to a laundry list of rules and rituals. That confines faith in the most unfortunate way. I have always viewed my faith as much more than just a body of rules and my community more than a group of people who adhere to the same rules. This faith took hold because of the efforts of people who were willing to be different, people who sought social justice and inspired a following by setting an example. To me, my faith represents an ideology that promotes self-development and a supportive community dedicated to promoting positive goals such as diversity, inclusion, discipline, resilience, and learning. Not only is exclusion not a tenet of the faith, it is directly contradictory to my understanding of Islam.

I'm a firm believer in individual journeys. I found wearing the headscarf insightful as to who I was, what being a woman meant, and how others perceived me. It was a lesson I frankly could not have fully appreciated without having chosen to experience both wearing hijab and not wearing hijab and seeing first hand how it changed perceptions around me – of myself, of my peers, and of my community. My current faith is so much stronger for the winding journey it took to get here. I wouldn't dare deny someone else the opportunity to navigate their own journey, to gauge their own level of commitment, and assess and reassess who they are, who they want to become, and how faith may play a role in that development.

I've never known of any faith-based or cultural community in which every single member has practised or represented it the same exact way. I imagine many communities face the struggle we're undergoing now. It's a struggle that superficially seems to be a battle between tradition and modern ways. But, at its core, it's actually a battle for whether a community will increasingly become exclusive or inclusive. My concern about how our community treats hijab represents my larger concern about the role we play in facilitating the development of our members. We must use our gatherings as a welcoming, safe space for people to come as they are. My fear is that we are evolving away from the very essence of what community should mean by imposing arbitrary barriers to entry and distinguishing insiders from outsiders.

For me, the question of how we address hijab, and women who choose to observe it in a particular way or not, says a lot about the kind of community we are and the kind of community we are evolving into. It is not solely an issue of hijab but about much larger issues of access and acceptance. It is about the Islamic concept of *da'wah* (inviting people to Islam), and whether we are getting more caught up in managing the entire community's *practice* of the faith rather than their *underlying understanding* of it. Today, kids are facing a lot more temptations and tougher choices at earlier ages than I ever did. They need safe spaces and alternative support systems to cope with a rapidly changing world in which they grow up faster than ever before. But if the purported alternative just offers yet another mandatory set of societal expectations (read: rules about fitting in) and the prospect of more alienation, the alternative is not truly an alternative, but just more of the same.

***

I wrote this piece more than two years ago. In an interesting twist, I have since decided to wear the headscarf again. This time, it wasn't about seeking cover from anything external, but having my outsides match my insides – meaning that I was ready publicly and visibly to identify as a Muslim woman and felt that the headscarf served as a daily reminder and marker of my beliefs, my willingness to stand up for them, and my defiance of the prevailing hateful narratives. It is a very different experience donning the scarf as an adult and in a time when articles of faith are extremely politicized. It doesn't change any part of what I wrote two years ago. Now, more than ever, we need to come together as a community and support our people, the ones that cover and the ones that don't. Today, the *cover* our community needs to be thinking about is creating a safe-space for all to contemplate and reflect upon our shared identities and struggles. The hope is that we, as a community, can provide that cover and start making genuine strides towards the theme of that conference so very long ago: unity and diversity.

Khawater al-Hijab — Thoughts on Hijab
Carrie York Al-Karam

"Allah does not look at your appearances or your financial status, but He looks at your hearts and your actions."
~Prophet Mohammed (Peace Be Upon Him)

When my stepdaughter was a young teenager and wanted to meet friends at the mall in Abu Dhabi, where we lived at that time, her father would always ask her who exactly she was going to meet there. Her description of her friends always included criteria like nationality (usually Syrian, Jordanian, or Palestinian), profession of the parents (usually the father), and whether or not the girl wore hijab. The hijab factor was always used to indicate that the girl was good friendship material and therefore worthy of going to the mall with.

My stepdaughter is not the only one whom I have heard make such assertions. I've heard them many times over the nearly thirteen years I lived in the Middle East, ten years of which were in the UAE. This assumption that a girl who wears hijab is "good" has always bothered me and as a result, has spurred many conversations with different people on numerous occasions.

What I have come to understand is this: wearing the hijab does not necessarily have anything to do with the quality of a woman's character or her level of faith. I arrived at this conclusion as a result of nearly two decades of lived experience with Muslims and after having been intricately embedded within various Islamic cultures for the majority of my adult life. I have also been a practising Muslim since 1999. I am married to a wonderful and devout Iraqi Muslim, and I have a degree in Middle East Studies, specializing in the topic of Muslim identity. As such, I have come to know many veiled and unveiled Muslim women over the years. Those women have possessed all types of personalities and have had all levels of faith. Some were religious, others not so much. What I can say about my experience with all of them is that I could not predict by any means whatsoever the type or quality of her character based simply on whether or not she wore the hijab.

Let me elaborate. I have personally known women who wore hijab yet engaged in *haram* romantic and sometimes sexual relationships with men. I have known veiled women who did not pray regularly or in some cases didn't pray at all. I have also known veiled women who gossiped regularly and intentionally tried to cause trouble amongst family members. One needs only to walk around a mall in any major city in the Arabian Gulf to see groups of *muhajibaats* (veiled women) strolling around for men with their flowing-open *abaya*s and half-way hijabs! On the other hand, I have also known veiled women who were very pious, with hijab being just one sign of their commitment to God and modesty. Indeed, many of my beloved Iraqi in-laws wear the hijab, including my mother-in-law, who is a deeply committed Muslim and a very dear person to me. As a Quran teacher, she imparts important religious and cultural knowledge to my five year-old daughter that might otherwise be lost, as I come from a white American background. I honour and respect her views on hijab and subsequent application of what she believes about it in her life, even if I might see things somewhat differently.

What I am trying to argue is that, at face value, the hijab is meaningless in terms of conveying the *type* of person the woman is. Unfortunately, my experience has taught me that judgments and conclusions are made about women based on the mere presence or absence of this otherwise neutral piece of headwear. It is often assumed that a veiled woman is a "good girl" — respectable and obedient to God and committed to her religion. Unveiled women, on the other hand, are suspect, their level of faith questioned by what some understand to be their disobedience of God's orders for her to wear the hijab. This judgment of a book by its cover is both unfortunate and unfair.

Muslim women and girls, as I have come to learn, wear hijab for a number of reasons. Some are required to do so by their families. Some wear it out of respect for local tradition. Some feel it is their duty to God, while others wear it to give the impression that they are pious. Of course, some wear it just to be fashionable! What I'm trying to say is that the reasons cannot be known by merely looking at a woman in a headscarf. Too often people assume that it is worn for the "right reasons". But it is important to keep in mind that hijab, in and of itself, cannot be a reliable indicator of the quality of character or level of faith, especially in countries where it's mandatory, can it? In my experience, the only thing I have ever been able to ascertain about a young girl who wears hijab is something about her *parents,* not her!

What is so ironic about the experience with my stepdaughter is that neither she nor I wear hijab. Considering that hijab was one criterion that my stepdaughter always brought up when trying to alleviate her father's concerns about the kinds of girls with whom she was hanging out, I have often wondered aloud what the other girls would tell their parents about her or our family. Were we deemed to have little faith, questionable morals, and low integrity? Was my stepdaughter not good enough to go to the mall with? What did we, as non-veiled females in a Muslim country, imply about my husband as the leader of the family, who has an impeccable reputation amongst those who know him and is a deeply committed Muslim?

I have had numerous personal experiences in which I was deemed "less than" for not wearing hijab. I have even had Muslims say to me that I will only be *kamil* (complete) once I wear it. As an adult with a pretty healthy sense of self, I can manage society's projections on me. But what about a young girl who grows up constantly being fed the belief that something is just not quite right with her and won't be until she wears hijab? In my experience in the Middle East, this is a common occurrence. I wish people understood how psychologically damaging it can be for families and societies to poison a girl's already fragile sense of self by equating her worth solely with wearing a headscarf. I fully support one of the underlying lessons that hijab is meant to teach – modesty. I think Western societies would be better off if more individuals adhered to this principle. I certainly try my best to comport myself with modesty in both my clothes and my behaviour. The latter actually encompasses the fuller meaning of hijab — not just wearing a headscarf, but behaving in ways that promote modesty. Unfortunately, it is the superficial aspect of hijab — the wearing of the headscarf — that gets all the attention, with very little attention paid to the deeper aspects of its meaning.

Reflections on the Hijab: Choice or Obligation?
Laila S. Dahan

> *"May your choices reflect your hopes not your fears."*
> ~Nelson Mandela

"Cover your hair!" is an oft-cited line in Hollywood versions of the Arab or Muslim world. Remember the film *Protocol* with Goldie Hawn? It was back in the early 1980s, and I recall that particular line because I had never personally heard it directed at any woman I knew. That changed when I spent time with my now ex-mother-in-law in a small town in Jordan back in the late 1990s. Some man had arrived at her home, and she actually told me to cover my hair! It was a first. I had spent a lifetime in Arab countries: Libya for fifteen years, Morocco for over a year, and the United Arab Emirates for over seventeen years. And in all those places, over all those years, no one had ever asked me to cover my hair.

In my experience, hijab and veiling continue to be strongly influenced by culture, politics, and family more than any religious edict. In Jordan, especially in the smaller towns outside the capital of Amman, families are strongly tied to cultural traditions. How the veil is used and perceived in a Muslim country depends not only on religious opinions, but on who is ruling the country, who has influence, and whether or not men are feeling that women somehow have too much – or any – power. This leads to what I call "oppressive veiling." You need only look at Iran, Afghanistan, and even parts of Iraq today as examples of men using the veil as a form of oppression and control.

It is unfortunate that this one aspect of Islam tends to be the focal point for both those inside and beyond the Muslim world. Frankly, I believe that most non-Muslim Westerners know very little about what Islam expects from its believers, but many of them have opinions nonetheless, especially about the hijab. When I refer to the West or Westerners, I am talking about countries such as the US, Canada, and most European nations where Muslims are the minority. As Theodore Gabriel (2011) points out, much of the debate in the "media, by politicians, and by the general public, is not well informed, does not fully consider all aspects of the issue and does not examine what the religion of Islam says about the dress of men and women" (p. 12). As such, Westerners tend to over-simplify the conversation by viewing the hijab as a symbol of oppression or believing the headscarf is a requirement for all Muslim women. This is evidenced by many television newscasts and documentaries about women in Islam, and in 2016, the rhetoric of a US presidential candidate. As this is a topic which continues to be so controversial even amongst Muslims, it is sometimes aggravating to see and hear so many Westerners join in the fray, even when they have no clue!

Examples of this in my own life are many. Often when I meet Westerners and they discover I am a Muslim, they are surprised that I don't wear the hijab, or Islamic headscarf. This is based on their understanding that "all Muslim women have to wear a head-covering." They ask if I face conflicts or negative issues from other Muslims because I choose not to wear it, which is ironic because I haven't faced any problems from other Muslims for not wearing a headscarf. Among the people I know, hijab is a personal issue unless a woman comes from a country or culture where it is forced upon her, like in Saudi Arabia, Iran, or Afghanistan, for example. I have had interesting debates, but I personally have never encountered a problem with other Muslims because I do not cover my hair. When I discuss this topic with non-Muslims, however, it is often quite clear from their responses or facial expressions that the nuances of my argument are lost. I can understand to some extent because I realize they do not have the same contexts from which to base their understanding and because the stereotype of the covered-up Muslim woman is rampant in film and television. It is rare for Western media to acknowledge that more than one type of Muslim woman exists. Considering the immense cultural diversity of Islam as a world religion, how often do we actually see a diverse representation of Muslim women in the media? Instead, the dominant image of the veiled woman results in the erasure of the multiple identities of real Muslim women (Bullock, 2011). We are essentially obliterated as real human beings!

I often wonder why it is that people who have done very little research about the Muslim world think they have carte blanche to pontificate on the reasons behind the hijab or the meaning of hijab. A prime example in 2016 was the Republican candidate for US president, Donald Trump. When Trump responded to the words of a Muslim Gold Star family, he said the mother (who wears a headscarf) did not speak perhaps because "she wasn't allowed to." In this instance, Trump, whose words were heard all over the world, put out the notion that a Muslim woman might "not be allowed to speak." The arrogance of this stance is hard to dismiss, but it feeds into the stereotypical dialogue surrounding Muslim women in American media. Muslim women have the right to speak out, but we also have the choice not to, as this mother did. In the same vein, we have the right to cover our hair, but we also have the choice not to! Certainly we can say that no one should listen to those who are not educated on the subject or have not researched the issue; however, many non-Muslim Westerners have no other source of information on this topic. They believe what they hear on the news and on television. As Omidvar and Richards (2014) point out, people with no real background about Islam or the hijab can be found on a number of media forums making claims that they pretend are true and valid, when very often they are only spewing stereotypes, devoid of any facts.

One might ask how I know they are making claims which are not true. I know because I am a Muslim woman. I know because I have studied Islam, not just as a Muslim, but as a scholar. The continual use of stereotypes against Muslims and Arabs has been well-documented (see for example, Alsultany, 2008; Said, 1981; Shaheen, 2001), and those stereotypes continue to be perpetuated, especially since the events of 9/11 in the United States.

As a Muslim woman who chooses not to veil, I am quite aware that part of my rationale for this choice is based on how I was raised, and the cultural milieu in which I grew up in Libya. My father was Muslim, my mother Baptist. She never converted and we celebrated all religious holidays, Muslim and Christian. Our beliefs and our religious convictions were carried within us, and not something my father or mother thought we needed to show the world by doing something as overt as covering our hair. My father did not interpret the Quran as requiring the hijab, although many of his family members did cover. However, the topic was not discussed in our home, or among our immediate family. Our values and beliefs guided how we lived our lives and how we managed ourselves in public. Those behaviors were far more important than what we did with our hair.

However, it would be remiss of me to disregard those women who have chosen to wear the headscarf based on a belief that this is what is required of them. British journalist Yasmin Alibhai-Brown says that many women who don the hijab of their own volition do so without questioning or researching the history and implications that are associated with this issue. As a Muslim woman, I have had many conversations with young women who veil. Some of these women have been my own relatives, others have been my students. As an academic, I spend time trying to understand why young women make certain decisions. I have personally seen how many young Muslim women wear the headscarf because their mother does or their father demands it or they are convinced by the society in which they live or the groups to which they belong. In most of the discussions I have had with these youg women, very few of them could cite a precise source in the Quran which justifies why they wear the hijab.

It is because of how I was raised that I have grown up not wearing the headscarf or ever even considering it. This is how Islam, especially with regard to the hijab, tends to be within Muslim families — much of it is personal, some of it is cultural and traditional. However, the one thing that is certain is that there are a great many interpretations of whether covering the hair is in fact an edict or an option for Muslim women. There are many who will argue at length that it is definitely a requirement, that those of us without the headscarf are doing something wrong or *haram*. However, as an academic, and before that a conscientious reader, I cannot accept that belief. I have read the Quran, I have seen how clear it is on most requirements, and then I get to the vagueness of the Surahs about the hijab, and it just doesn't resonate with me as an imperative. I fail to see the decree.

The main problem about the issue of veiling, from my perspective, is how this *rule* about the hijab has been (mis)interpreted by so many people, Muslims and non-Muslims alike. It seems fairly clear that mandatory regulations of Islam are very openly addressed in the Quran. There is no confusion over alcohol or pork. Yet, the sections of the Quran employed by those who claim that the headscarf is mandatory, first of all, refer to the wives of the Prophet, and second, never contain the word "hair" or "head".

There are two Quranic citations which are at the center of the debate on whether hijab is about wearing a veil or more generally about modesty. The first is Surah 33:59, which was addressed to the Prophet Muhammad and his family, indicating that his wives and daughters should wear outer garments in order to be "known" (meaning recognized). Although hijab has become equated with the Islamic headscraft, the term "hijab" literally means "screen", which refers to the etiquette required for interaction with the Prophet's wives (Zahedi, 2007). Given the public nature of the Prophet's work in a patriarchal Arab society circa

600 AD, the edict was an important reminder to Muslim men to provide the Prophet's family with some level of privacy. It also substantiates the point that other women of that time period were not veiled (Zahedi, 2007). The other is Surah 24:31 which emphasizes modesty for men and women and instructs Muslim women to cover their bosom and neck with the *khimr*, the scarf that many women at the time wore on their head, while often leaving their breasts exposed. There is no specific mandate in this Surah for covering women's hair. If a Muslim woman covers her hair in allegiance with the cultural norms of the Arab world during the time of the Prophet, that is certainly her right to do so, but does it make hair cover a mandatory element for all women who consider themselves to be practicing Muslims?

It is at this point that one really needs to question the conviction that these specific sections of the Quran have the meaning some maintain they do. If these pieces of the Quran were as straightforward as all other segments, it would not require all this "interpretation". The words are just not there, nothing about heads or hair. Instead the passages discuss modesty, and one is directed to the Prophet's family and not the general public. A factor we must keep in mind is that anytime we are reading religious texts, there will always be different interpretations and understandings. This allows for flexibility with regard to what practicing Muslim women may consider as modest or compulsory. The interpretation of these religious texts are also influenced by the time and place in which people live. Muslim women have been living under a patriarchal reading and interpretation of Islamic texts and this is something which is beginning to change. In my case, it already has changed how I understand the issue of hijab.

In addition to my own view that wearing the headscarf is voluntary, I have also witnessed many instances when it seems to be donned because a woman's parents or family is forcing it upon her. This is in contradiction to Islam, which is very clear that compulsion should not be a part of religion; we cannot force things upon others. Compulsion can result in people following the letter of the law, while ignoring what the religion actually has to say. I have seen this with young women in both Jordan and the UAE who take great care to cover their hair, yet wear clothing so tight and figure-hugging that every outline of their bodies is revealed. They carefully cover from the chin up, only to share with the world all the curves below. This seems in direct conflict to the entire discussion of modesty in the Quran, which is at the heart of the argument. Is hijab about maintaining modesty in our choice of clothing or is it only about covering the hair?

I have had this topic come up in my university classrooms, and while some students are lecturing their peers on the necessity of the headscarf, I have asked male students, "Are men really looking at women's hair or are you looking at other things?" I have gotten some nervous laughter from this query, some groans of embarrassment, and some young men saying pleadingly, "Oh, Miss!" In the discussions that followed, students, both male and female, agreed that most often men are far more interested in the female physique below the chin, rather than the crowning glory atop our heads.

But all of their horrified expressions and objections point to the reality of the function of the headscarf, especially in a world in which some young women are more interested in keeping up with modern fashion, tight as it may be, than ensuring that the idea of hijab is upheld. Sure, covering the hair is not a problem, as long as they can still wear skinny jeans and tight t-shirts. Furthermore, I have seen young women arriving from Saudi Arabia to other Arab countries and immediately shedding their headscarves. As the law of Saudi Arabia decrees that women must wear the headscarf, it is very much imposed on them. Once they are out of reach of Saudi norms, many of these young women feel they are no longer under the obligation to cover their hair. If they are not wearing the hijab by choice, then once outside the borders, it is not surprising that they wouldn't feel the need to follow the rules laid out by their country's leadership.

Another issue that arises regarding the hijab is whether or not it truly protects women from the gazes or lewd comments of men. Let's take women in Egypt as an example. The Egyptian Centre for Women's Rights argues that over 80 percent of Egyptian females have been harassed (Alibhai-Brown, 2014). Women wearing the hijab in Cairo have been chased, molested, and had their scarves removed by men intent on touching women - apparently any women - even those who by virtue of their hijab are intending to give a clear signal that they are modest, and in the opinion of some, more modest than those of us who don't cover. Therefore, we see in this situation that the hijab is not the protective garment it is intended to be. The term "protective" refers to the belief that women who wear the hijab are less apt to be exploited for their beauty as they are seeking to de-sexualize their worth as human beings. Unfortunately, despite women wearing it, they are still harassed by men.

I had a Muslim-American friend with quite pale skin and bright blue eyes who told me that wearing the hijab in the Arab world failed to protect her from vulgar comments from men. She was accosted by men on more than one occasion. Apparently, because she does not look dark enough or Arab enough to be Muslim - another stereotype - her hijab did little to protect her from improper comments. It is these types of factors which contribute to my own disillusionment with the power given to the hijab, both in terms of being worn by women who supposedly are more religious or pious than those of us who don't wear it and because it still does not stop some men from acting inappropriately when they are supposed to look upon all women, but especially veiled women, as "sisters" who should be protected.

I am a firm believer in the right to choose. Unfortunately, freedom of choice when it comes to religious views, beliefs, and interpretations is a rare commodity. I am mindful that I grew up in a home that acknowledged and supported the differences found within it, and I am thankful every day for the openness in which I was raised. As a Muslim woman who chooses not to wear the hijab, it is not my place to tell women who don the headscarf to remove it because of my beliefs and interpretations. And so I worry about young Muslim women today who are lectured by their society, their families, and other women to prove their Islamic convictions by wearing the headscarf. This bothers me because I do not like to see the interpretations of some pushed upon others. However, until women in the Muslim world are able to attain more rights to self-determination, this notion of wearing the hijab will remain a subject of controversy. My hope is that Muslim women will continue to strive for their rights, and in so doing be allowed to make their own decisions to veil or not to veil.

References

Alibhai-Brown, Y. (2014). *Refusing the veil*. London: Biteback Publishing, Ltd.

Alsultany, E. (2008). The prime-time plight of the Arab Muslim American after 9/11: Configurations of race and nation in TV dramas. In A. Jamal & N. Naber (Eds.), *Race and Arab Americans before and after 9/11: From invisible citizens to visible subjects*, (pp. 204-228). Syracuse, NY: Syracuse

University Press.

Bullock, K. (2011). Hijab and belonging: Canadian Muslim women. In T. Gabriel & R. Hannan (Eds.), *Islam and the veil: Theoretical and regional contexts,* (pp.161-180). London & New York: Continuum International Publishing Group.

Gabriel, T. (2011). Reflections on sartorial injunctions in Islam. In T. Gabriel & R. Hannan (Eds.), *Islam and the veil: Theoretical and regional contexts,* (pp.12-19). London & New York: Continuum International Publishing Group.

Omidvar, I., & Richards, A.R. (Eds.). (2014). *Muslims and American popular culture:Volume one: Entertainment and digital culture.* Santa Barbara, CA: Praeger.

Said, E.W. (1981). *Covering Islam: How the media and the experts determine how we see the rest of the world.* New York: Vintage Books.

Shaheen, J.G. (2001). *Reel bad Arabs: How Hollywood vilifies a people.* New York: Olive Branch Press.

Zahedi, A. (2007). Contested meaning of the veil and political ideologies of Iranian regimes. *Journal of Middle East Women's Studies, 3*(3), 75-98.

PART 5

THE PURSUIT OF SENTIENCE

Reflections on the Veil: An art work in Yemen and an experiment in Germany

Angelika Böck

> *"When we love a work of art, there is always a form of recognition*
> *that occurs. The object reflects us, not the way a mirror gives our*
> *faces and bodies back to us. It reflects the vision of the other, of the*
> *artist, that we have made our own because it answers something*
> *within us that we understand is true."*
>
> ~Siri Hustvedt

The shopkeeper helped me button up the *abaya* that my assistant, Basmah, had chosen for me. It consisted of a loose full-length black coat-like garment with sleeves that appeared much too long for my taste. I put on the black gloves and stockings she held out to me. Then she helped me to wrap a long narrow shawl of black material around my head in such a way that my hair and the upper part of my face were covered down to my eye lashes. She attached a ribboned rectangular piece of cloth, which she tied behind my ears. It fell in front of my face from the lower eye lid down over my breast. I looked into the mirror. All that was left visible of me were my eyes and nose bridge. I had the impression that the woman had pulled the material too close to my eyes and so I adjusted it. My assistant frowned. It was how I was supposed to wear the stuff, Basmah told me, and turned to say something in Arabic to the shopkeeper. The lady opened a drawer and brought out a large piece of black double layered semi-see-through material which she pulled over my head and shoulders and buttoned in front of my chest so that it formed a kind of hood. She folded the outer layer of the hood back over my head and shoulders. The now one-layered material, that covered my eyes, was as dense as 40 den stockings. I could barely see. When I caught sight of my obscured self in the mirror, I laughed out loud. I was reminded of myself playing ghost as a child under a bedsheet — only in black.

My assistant smiled, satisfied. "You will have to wear this, otherwise your green eyes and white skin will give you away."

Her task was to make me unrecognizable as a foreigner and she only did her job, but I could hardly breathe when we left the air-conditioned shop and went out into the heat of the day. Within seconds the bottom of my coat caught the dust from the street while Basmah, who was wearing an *abaya* and a headscarf, stayed clean. She said, "You have to take smaller steps."

I didn't feel invisible, as I had imagined I would, and thought everyone must see what a cheat I was. Then I realized that no one was looking at me any longer. When we stopped at a market stall to buy a pair of stockings, the male seller kept his head bowed during the exchange.

I had come to Sana'a, the capital of Yemen, to carry out an art project on the veil. I had visited the country two years earlier and my interest in the veil had been triggered by our driver, who had suddenly cried out in excitement when we passed a group of veiled women, "Among one hundred women I am able to recognize my sister!" I was astonished by this certainty and started to wonder whether an experienced observer — a normal Yemeni person — would not only be able to recognize a familiar woman, but be capable of attributing looks and character to a stranger behind her veils.

Angelika Böck in the process of carrying out *Imagine Me* in Sana'a
Photo by Thomas Barnstein

Disguised as a Yemeni woman, I approached thirty respondents in Sana'a with the help of two research assistants, Arwa and Samah, two young Yemeni women who had both studied the German language. I challenged the onlookers to observe me very carefully, and asked them later to describe my looks, character and personal circumstances. The interviews took place in private as well as in public, and were carried out in two different ways. In the public space, my assistants searched for men willing to participate before they beckoned me to come closer. In private surroundings, we arrived together and they directed me by hand signals. In the latter cases, the respondents were already prepared for an interview situation by a mediator. All statements were recorded. After the enquiry, in private, I revealed my identity and requested a photo of the interviewee. The photos of the men that were contacted in the street were taken at a second meeting arranged by the interviewer at the end of the session. These portraits were usually made the next day at the interviewee's home, office or shop, and their statements were later translated into German.

Two respondents in Yemen
Photos courtesy of Angelika Böck

Sixteen quotes were selected for the *Imagine Me* display, which was a cubic structure covered with black cloth and twenty-five photo portraits.

An old merchant at the Souq said, "The woman looks good. Only God knows who she is."

A young mistress remarked, "This woman could be a man. She is educated and certainly works. She is neither rich nor poor. She's about 20 years old. "

An elderly businessman thought, "This woman is definitely no housewife. She has completed her studies and works. She is confident, independent and eager. She is not rich, has a mobile phone but no car. She does what she wants and maintains an opinion. She is a believing Muslim but not a devout one. She loves nature and everything beautiful. She hates violence. Her parents were often disputing. She has beautiful eyes and a nice nose, medium-length black hair and light skin. She loves to sing under the shower. She is reasonably healthy. She has no children yet. She is between 20 and 30 years old."

A middle-aged tradesman observed, "This woman is not handsome. She walks like a mannequin or soldier. She is poor and without interest. She is unreliable, messy and badly organized. She is not a good housewife. She has little chance of getting husband and a house. She has a good body without doing anything for it. Her face is neither beautiful nor ugly. "

A middle-aged confectioner remarked, "This woman walks like a woman from Sana'a, dresses like one from Taiz, but doesn't look like a Yemeni. She is gorgeous! She is educated and very pretty. She gets scared easily. She has blue eyes and white skin. She is of middle age."

An elderly housewife declared, "This woman is like all the others. She has not much money. She leads a simple life."

An old writer said, "The woman looks like a ghost under this black hull. She originates from a Yemeni middle-class family, seems to have studied at the university, and works. Through her mute participation in this project she possibly wants to demonstrate a thesis. Her way of walking tells of her propensity towards violence. Under the cover of calmness she might hide her emotions. She has black eyes and hair but light skin. She is certainly fashionable. She is totally healthy."

All of these statements reflected the imagined being who was behind the veil.

The *Imagine Me* Display in Sana'a, Yemen
Photo courtesy of Angelika Böck

Imagine Me is an art work that is part of *Portrait as Dialogue*, a practice-based research project which aims to develop a critical approach to representation based on primary fieldwork. It addresses the question of how we can identify with the depictions or descriptions of our *selves* that are created from *other* cultural perspectives. The major focus is to understand how specific forms of representation could reveal differently authored perceptions of the individual – in this case, the individual behind the veil.

In Sana'a, the inaccessible corpus was placed in the centre of the exhibition space. Four black textile panes were tacked onto each side. On each cloth a text was embroidered in German and Arabic using golden thread. Each pane represented one of the sixteen selected interviews. The dark material of the display referred to the *abaya*; the golden color represented the female jewellery. The photos were taken as snapshots. On each wall surrounding the cube, the portraits of the participants that allowed their picture to be taken were hung. There was no direct correspondence between the image and the quotation.

I was later asked how West European respondents might have interpreted a veiled appeareance in a similar setting. The question made me curious. I decided to carry out a small experiment — not as an art work but as inspiration for research — and persuaded my mother to put on my Yemeni disguise. In Maximilianstrasse in Munich, where the veiled female body is widely represented by shopping Arab women, I approached various pedestrians of different sexes and ages (most of them were of German nationality) with the same question posed in Sana'a. My mother kept strictly at such a distance to me that my conversation partner could eye her well without fearing she would hear his or her answer. Unlike the Yemeni interviewees, who seemed to have no difficulty in using their own senses and imagination to describe a veiled woman, none of the fifteen respondents were able to respond to the task.

The interviewees' gazes seemed unable to capture an image beyond the veil. Instead, most respondents commented – unasked — about the veil itself and the life the veiled women supposedly led. This would have been unthinkable in the Yemeni context. Their short answers often contained more or less politely formulated damnation, incomprehension, pity, or mistrust. On occasion tolerance was expressed.

Elfriede, a 72-year old respondent, ventured, "The woman is perhaps fifty years old and leads, at home in their harem, a normal life. She doesn't act suppressed."

A 48-year old woman, Elvira, noted, "I disagree with the fact that women obscure themselves. I want to see people in the eye and recognize their body language. This is very important for me. These people do not let us near them. That scares me."

Eva, a 32-year old woman, exclaimed, "You cannot see anything from the woman, not a face, not even her eyes. The veil completely covers her individuality. I often feel sorry for these women."

Marianne, a 71-year woman, agreed. "When I see someone like that, I feel sorry. Especially when I imagine that the woman must be dressed so in a hot country. That is cruel. But you cannot help them. It will be like this for another hundred years to come. But some women are also very confident — there is of course money behind it."

Fritz, a 79-year old man, said "Only Iranian women are so fully veiled. It does not fit, in any case, with the cityscape here, and that already starts with the headscarf."

A 40-year old woman, Irene, stated, "You never know who is under such a garment. It might be a man. It is difficult for me to imagine that the women wear it voluntarily. I would not walk around like that. I think it's rude."

Interview in Maximilianstrasse, Munich, in 2009
Photo: Thomas Barnstein, courtesy of Angelika Böck

And Eckhart, a 78-year old respondent, replied, "All I register is a black-clad lady. How she looks like under this veil, I cannot imagine. "

Whereas the Middle Eastern imagination was able to permeate the veil, the Westerners had no way around it!

The material presented by *Imagine Me* was dependent on many decisions, consciously or or unconsciously made, which may have influenced the responses given. The driver who inspired the project may have recognized his sister because he was driving on a street that she frequently crossed. Perhaps the recognition was based on a similar body shape, movement or accessory, or it might have simply been a result of wishful thinking. My mediators may have purposely chosen participants in Yemen who had a certain view on women or the veil or might have involuntarily revealed information about it being a stranger who initated the project by using herself as the object of the study. The interviewers may have pushed the responses into a certain direction with their questions and my assistants may have translated, out of politeness, unfavourable responses in a moderate manner. And, last but not least, I shortened the translated quotations and selected those which appeared the most interesting to me, and these were later retranslated into the Arabic language.

My aim is not to make binding, lasting claims about the veil. Rather, I am interested in visualizing a question together with reflections on a given subject. To this end I use my own experiences as well as the experiences of others in order to get a better understanding of myself and of the world around me.

The Veil and the American Belly Dancer
Carol Tandava Henning

> *" [U]nveiling suggests a need to be utterly exposed, undefended, open to having one's soul searched by the dark eye of the Self the end of one form of body-ego existence and the revelation of the hidden Self."*
> ~Sylvia Brinton Perera

"Unveiling", "Unveiled", "Behind the Veil", "Beyond the Veil", "Dances with Veils", and my own "Blood on the Veil" – in books, DVDs, music, theatre, the veil is synonymous with the belly dance in American culture. Its diaphanous presence surrounds the art form in idea and practice, highlighting the fluid movements of the dancer's body, or enrapturing the audience with its own dynamic swirls and tricks. It is practically a cliché: Even "belly dancer" Halloween costumes contain either a full veil, or a small square of sheer fabric draped beneath the eyes or framing the face á *la I Dream of Jeannie*.

Salome's notorious "Dance of the Seven Veils" has infused the Western imagination for over a century, first conjured by Oscar Wilde's 1891 play *Salomé,* in which the eponymous lady dances for her uncle, King Herod, in exchange for the head of John the Baptist. The actual Biblical tale, however, does not mention what kind of dance she did, or whether or not any fabric was involved – or even that her name was Salomé. But the scene has been represented in opera, film and theater, by countless belly dancers, and even parodied on television shows like the 1960s' *Batman.*

The veil is the quintessential prop in cabaret-style belly dance. If the dancer does not perform her first number with the veil, she will use it as a clever wrap to hide her costume. Then when the slower, more sensuous music of the second song begins, she will gradually remove the veil, revealing the costume and further enchanting the crowd with magical swirls, billows, ripples, flutters, and flourishes. As a novice dancer, it quickly became my favorite prop. Simply holding it behind my body gave me a sense of grandeur and luxury. And as I learned to navigate the fabric around my form, feeling it catch the air then slither across my skin, it seemed less of a prop and more of a partner.

Clichés notwithstanding, the veil is quintessentially feminine. At an archetypal level, the feminine is that which is hidden. It is the mysterious, that which is unknown but beckoning to be grasped. It is a siren call over water, irresistibly luring towards excitement, vitality, even danger.

And as a dancer, the veil enables me to embody this powerful symbolism. Draped around my body in a "veil wrap", the piece of cloth covers, hides and casts my figure into mystery. Pinned to one shoulder, the fabric cascades like a toga, hinting at the image of an ancient goddess. With the long rectangle pulled over my head, the fabric covers me completely – and yet this is the most revealing of the veil wraps because it leaves the costume's outline clearly visible.

One of my favourite entrances is to approach with my arms stretched to the sides, or in a prayer position in front of the fabric. And as I walk forward, the silk presses into my costume, showing its contours and decorations. Then, I take a step backward, pulling the fabric away. Suddenly the image is lost. As the music builds momentum, I repeat these moves, giving the audience several minutes to imagine what the costume will be. The final unveiling can be a gradual peeling away, letting the reality catch up to the imagination. Or it can be a fast swish, a dramatic shock to contrast with the initial languidness.

This component of the performance can be very sensual, and can invoke Salomé's iconic strip tease – but not as a sexual enticement towards men. The concept of a female gradually removing garments dates back to ancient Mesopotamia, where the Sumerian goddess of love, fertility, and warfare – the Queen of Heaven, Inanna – descends to the underworld to visit her dark sister, Ereshkigal, the Queen of the Underworld. To gain entrance, Inanna is told to pass through seven gates. At each gate, she must remove a piece of clothing or jewelry – the outward symbols of her power – until she is stripped entirely. Her nakedness before her sister is not an allure to men (who only marginally appear in this myth); rather, her state represents one's unadorned, receptive, vulnerable self. It is only in this wholly authentic state that Inanna can connect with her dark sister, who is herself veiled by the earth's crust. Ereshkigal represents volcanic unconscious forces – the psychological womb from which creativity is borne – that are far stronger than the surface elements through which we define and identify ourselves. If we don't humbly relinquish our chosen veils of illusion in such an encounter, then they may be stripped from us.

Joseph Campbell, the American author and mythologist, said that mythologies were not intended to explain world's phenomena, but rather to give us a framework through which to understand our experience of ourselves and the world, and thereby put both inner and outer realities in accord with each other. A myth's greatest power is in its ability to inform even the most seemingly insignificant events. So at that moment of unveiling, even dancing in a little restaurant in the middle of nowhere, I invoke Inanna – slowly, carefully revealing my truest self, the part of myself that can receive and transmit music, emotion, passion, vitality through my body.

It is in this receptive state that I am most able to see the veil as a partner. Granted, there is a known vocabulary of "veil moves", each with its own descriptive name and technique – such as "matador switch", "butterfly", and "airplane" – and while I include many of these movements in choreographies and structured improvisations, I remain aware that the veil does not always follow my plans. Sometimes, it takes on a presence of its own. Like Inanna standing before her chthonic sister, I do my best humbly to let the veil take the lead, following as it catches puffs of air then swings into a grand cascade – creating not only stunning veil work but bringing a sense of transcendence, or *Tarab,* in my dance.

My first experiences with "dancing on *Tarab*" – allowing myself to be transported by the emotion of the music – were in Sufi workshops with masters including Adnan Sarhan, Dunya, and Nahari. We were encouraged simply to hold the veil in front of us as the music permeated the room and our bodies, and then simply to allow the veil to "catch" the music, to let it lead us in movement, to let it mesmerize us with its shimmering waves and undulations, to let it bring us to a state of transcendence. To touch this ecstatic state in performance is transformational for both the dancer and audience.

And as the veil helped me take flight, so it helps me return, settling into a drape framing my hips, torso, or face, recalling the wrap in which I entered. Another kind of "frame" is called "the envelope", in which I fold the long rectangle widthwise and hold it above my head, so my torso and arms are completely covered. From this position, the opening at the top can be brought forward and down until it reaches my eyes. If I pull back, I create the wrap sometimes called "Arab Woman". This is a makeshift *niqab* that obscures the entire upper body, except for the eyes.

This wrap is a favorite of American audiences, partly because it's done so quickly that it resembles a magic trick, and partly because it conjures that familiar image of Orientalist fantasy: the veiled but naked harem girl. For this reason, it is also a subject of debate among American dancers, who argue that it may cross a line in pandering to Orientalism, a romanticism of Middle Eastern culture that sexualizes and caricatures both women and Islamic dress. In my experience, however, Middle Eastern audience members (at least in the United States) do not respond negatively to this move, though I have not and probably would not try it with a wholly Middle Eastern audience, partly because I would worry that it may seem culturally offensive and partly because Middle Eastern audiences are less interested in veil tricks than Americans.

Melisula from the Phoenix production of *Blood on the Veil*, 8 April 2016
Photo Courtesy of Carol Tandava Henning

Ironically, in spite of the entrenched association of the veil with the "mysterious feminine of the Middle East", it is rarely used by Middle Eastern dancers, and was not a common feature in belly dance until the 1940s, when a famous Egyptian dancer named Samia Gamal was taught by her Russian ballet teacher to hold a piece of fabric behind her in order to improve her arm carriage. Today's Egyptian dancers, like many Middle Eastern dancers, simply use the veil to create an entrancing flourish, much in the way Liberace swept his cape around the stage before sitting at the piano. To them, it is nothing special, and does not seem to invoke any particular symbolism to either dancer or audience.

But in America it remains and continues to develop as an integral component to belly dance. In my own work, my goal is to explore the veil as both prop and partner, keeping in mind the ancient feminine symbolism it invokes in this culture – yet, through my studies with Middle Eastern teachers, remaining respectful to the culture in which my dance is rooted.

I Am My Hair
N.B. Sky

"I am not my hair
I am not this skin
I am not your expectations, no no
I am not my hair
I am not this skin
I am the soul that lives within"
~India Irie

I wish I was more like India Irie. Because, unlike her, I am my hair. I always have been. My hair is a direct reflection of me, both my vulnerabilities and my strengths. I use it as a display of my sexuality and sensuality. I wrap myself in it when I need cover and protection. It is my personal symbol of beauty. It is what sets me apart from others. It hides my personal story.

I am my hair. And I'm embarrassed to admit it.

My mother rocked long hair growing up and into adulthood. I remember hiding under her long, dark locks in our little apartment in Queens, New York, bombarding her with questions about what she did to make it grow. Her hair was my safety net. In my teen years, it was the barricade that kept out my father's frightening tirades. Under the cover of her thick strands, his flying fists seem farther away than they actually were. Her hair smelled like Sunday mornings – a mix of spices cooking on the stove, daffodils and coconut oil. The scent was a grateful reminder that Saturday night was over and we had survived another one of my father's drunken outbursts.

Over time, I began to associate hair with warmth, safety, sensuality and beauty. As I grew up, my hair grew with me. It became long and thick and the compliments I received on it were endless. In high school and college, everyone from hairdressers to family to strangers would constantly praise me for being the owner of such coveted hair. I was valuable because I possessed the "crowning glory" that so many women longed for. And so the belief was cultivated that my hair and my worth were one and the same, until I could no longer tell where my spirit ended and my hair began.

When I started studying Hinduism, the religion I was born into, I learned that hair is considered holy and should be protected and taken care of. My desire and appreciation for my hair only grew because I now saw it as symbolic, religious and necessary. I could flaunt my hair not just because it was attractive, but also because it was holy! So covering my hair for any spiritual purpose never even crossed my mind. Instead, it was through Indian cinema that I became aware of the power of veiling.

In my teens, I had a great appreciation for Bollywood dancing, through which a dupatta, or veil, is often used in a choreographed number. In Indian films, the dupatta plays a dual role. It represents modesty and shyness when the starlet appears on screen, eyes down, head covered, characterizing the treasured qualities of the traditional Indian woman. Yet when the scene changes, as it inevitably does, the veil transforms into a symbol of sensuality and seduction, undulating to the rhythm of the tabla and sitar. Were these two veils the same? Wearing the dupatta in my choreographed dances made me feel beautiful, mysterious and magical. Because of its dichotomous symbolism, I could perform in front of family members at an event, using the veil to portray the image of a sweet, innocent girl. But in front of friends, I could quickly and easily transform into an assertive, audacious woman – all through the use of this magical dupatta. And so the veil became an accessory that magnified the importance of my hair because hiding behind the translucent waves of the fabric, my hair was waiting to take center stage.

For about two decades, my life revolved around my appearance. I wanted to be seen - to be noticed, revered, and loved. I pulled, teased, lightened, curled and straightened my hair to look like those video vixens who appeared both in Hindi movies and in music videos on MTV. And it worked. I got the attention I wanted. But the attention never led to the genuine love and respect I sought so desperately. I received tons of compliments about my "beautiful" hair, but my self-esteem stagnated. I realized on some level that this had evolved from the experiences of my childhood. Even though I had worked hard to win my parents' approval, I constantly felt like I was never good enough. I always remained lacking, except when it came to my hair. And so, the belief solidified. I was certain that making myself attractive would bring me love and respect.

And then I met a man.

"Sweetheart, I love your hair. It's my solace. It makes me feel protected."

"When we make love, I love when it's all over my face. It makes me feel safe."

"I just want to hide in it. Don't ever cut it."

With those words, I felt that all my efforts had paid off. My hair had finally brought me what I needed. But then it changed. What started out as a reflection of love and desire slowly became a source of control and manipulation. My hair began to symbolize all that was going wrong with my relationship.

"Other men shouldn't be able to see your hair. It's for me only."

"I haven't yet required you to wrap your hair. Don't make me start doing that."

"When you leave the house, I want your hair tied up or in a braid. Don't let me see you outside of this house with your hair out."

One day, I went to the salon to get my hair trimmed. He decided he needed to see exactly what I had done to my hair and surprised me at my apartment that evening. He was upset that I had cut my hair two inches, appalled that I had dared to do something to my hair without his permission. Suddenly, I was brought back to that apartment in Queens where fists flew and I lived in fear of where they might land.

I never went to bed that night. The argument lasted until the early morning when the alarm clock told me it was time to get ready for work. I was exhausted and shocked at how my hair, this part of me that I loved so much, was suddenly being used against me. I couldn't fathom how my hair, which had always made me feel safe, was now bringing me so much pain. In that relationship, I was no longer the owner of my hair. He was. I was suffocating under the weight of a relationship that was becoming increasingly violent. I was reliving some of my worst experiences as a child, but this time I couldn't hide behind my mother's long locks. I couldn't even hide behind mine because my hair no longer belonged to me.

I was angry that this man felt he owned my hair and, through extension, my body and mind. Growing up, I had heard that it was the Muslim men who required their women to cover their hair. This was something of which I had always been convinced, yet, this man I was dating was not Muslim. Ironically, the man I was with previously was Muslim, yet he had never asked me to cover my hair. On the contrary, he had encouraged me to do what I liked with it. It became clear to me then that when a man tells a woman to cover her hair, it has less to do with religion and more to do with power and control.

Gratefully, several months later the toxic relationship imploded. I no longer needed to consult anyone on how to wear my hair. I could cut it short or wear it wild and curly. It was liberating for me to have control over my life and my body again, but it was also scary and complicated. I found myself questioning whether covering my hair would be good for me. I was becoming wary of the hold it had on me. The comments of admiration suddenly seemed to be tinged with a hint of envy. When strangers reached out to touch my hair, the feeling of being violated seared through my body. Why did people, especially men, think it was their right to touch my hair? On the train, in clubs, in restaurants and other places, my hair was touched uninvitingly and inappropriately by someone I didn't know. There were times when I had reprimanded the perpetrator, and other times when I thought it better to walk away for my safety. Covering my hair would keep that unwanted attention at bay. These ideas floated around in my mind, but I was no longer used to doing things according to my own will. I needed someone or something to tell me what to do.

I researched Hinduism again to look into what the religion says about how a woman's hair should be worn. Because the veil is so often romanticized in Indian cinema, I wondered if there was a religious aspect to the cultural practice. I learned that while hair is considered holy in Hinduism, covering it wasn't a requirement. So, I continued my exploration.

I researched Islam, and learned that Muslim women are often the ones to decide whether or not to cover their hair. While much of the world sees the hijab as a form of control and repression, I began to understand that many Muslim women prefer to cover their hair to maintain modesty and to restrain the ego. I had realized by this point how much I depended on my hair and my physical appearance for validation, so I was very interested in learning to restrain my ego. I toyed with the idea of covering my hair as a Muslim woman would.

Even now, the thought crosses my mind at times. While I have seriously considered it, I always become fearful of the questions and judgments I would have to face if I did so. Although I was once married to a Muslim man, I never converted to Islam. I worry that my family will question if I am covering my hair for sudden religious reasons related to that relationship. I'm nervous that my friends will think my ex's barbaric views are so deeply ingrained in me that they still influence my decisions. My co-workers will want to know the whole story and I'm just not ready to divulge those personal details to some.

I am newly single and I still associate my hair with beauty and sensuality. I still feel that I need my hair to entice and capture the attention of a man. I wish

I was strong enough to hide my hair and use my intelligence and humour for this endeavor, but unfortunately, these characteristics have always come in second to my hair. If my hair isn't on display, what would others notice about me? What would they initially like about me? Am I smart enough, funny enough, kind enough to keep someone's attention?

Who am I without my hair?

When I'm at my strongest, I can easily convince myself that covering my hair is the right thing for me to do. However, when that strength slips and I enter my daily reality, I realize that I still rely on my hair. It is my protection and my pride. While I feel like I have grown immensely as a person, my physical appearance continues to be important to me. Even though I'm in a better place in my life, I still struggle sometimes with that nagging voice in my head that tells me that maybe I'm not good enough.

I aspire to feel beautiful – to know I'm beautiful – whether my hair is covered, cut super short or long and flowing as it currently is. I want to feel confident and whole, regardless of how I look or what my hair is up to on any particular day. I realize that feeling beautiful needs to come from within me. I *am* more than my hair. But it is a struggle and a process which takes time, patience and a ton of self-love.

Tomorrow, I have a date. So, tonight, I will use my colour-safe shampoo to protect the hair I dyed two days ago to cover up the pesky hint of white that suddenly appeared at my crown. And, tomorrow morning, I will straighten my hair to ensure it is frizz-free and shiny. My journey towards self-love is ongoing and maybe one day my hair will be a less important part of that. But, for now, it is who I am and I'm learning to be okay with that.

Lifting the Veil on Islam in Hollywood
Kamran Pasha

> *"I have nothing against the veil. And I think that, wrongly, many in the West look at the veil as a symbol of oppression. Now, as long as a woman chooses to wear the veil, because that's her belief and because of her own — that's a personal relationship with God, so she should be free to dress in whichever way she wants."*
> ~Queen Rania of Jordan

Hollywood is an industry defined by visual images, and there is no image more arresting to the media than that of the veiled woman. The veil has come to symbolize in the media narrative all that is wrong with Islam. A simple strip of cloth has come to represent in the Western narrative the alleged misogyny and medieval cultural values of Muslims, and by subtly linking these values to broader issues of "honour killings" in parts of the Middle East, is used to strengthen the image of Islam as a violent and primitive religion.

And yet for a great many Muslim women, both in Muslim-majority countries as well as in the West, the veil represents completely opposite values. It is seen by many of those who wear it as a sign of spirituality, dignity and nobility. So the question arises as to why there is such a large variation between how the media presents the veil and how it is actually perceived by the Muslim women who wear it.

As a Muslim filmmaker who has worked in Hollywood for over fifteen years, I have been able to have direct insight as to how the media machine creates and controls the public narrative on Islam. And the examples of anti-Muslim bigotry I have experienced in the industry are quite shocking. Early in my career, I learned that a famous producer who had expressed interest in buying a script I had written telling the Crusades from the Muslim point of view actually sought to suppress the project and make sure it was never filmed. I remember taking notes from a respected TV executive who told me directly, "Don't make the villain of the episode Chinese. Make him Arab. Everybody hates them." I have sat in a writers' room on a television series and listened to a producer say, "The best way to solve the problem of terrorism is to kill Muslim children so they know we mean business." I remember trying to pitch a light-hearted action show while a network buyer kept going off on *non-sequiturs* about how "Muslims are trying to kill us all." Or the film executive who boasted proudly that he had removed a Cat Stevens song from a hit movie because Stevens (a Muslim convert) "supported terrorists" by means of his charity work in Palestine.

The distaste I have experienced toward Islam in general takes a very specific form when it addresses the veil. Many of the producers I have worked with in Hollywood see the veil as the defining proof of the backwardness of Islam in respect of women's issues. The veil becomes a lightning rod about how Islam is allegedly incompatible with the modern world — a message that they have sought to underline in the movies and televisions shows they produce. I have witnessed how those wishing to influence public policy toward the Muslim world have used the veil to symbolize in one quick image the impression they wish to create. But what I have also discovered is that the attitudes within Hollywood toward the veil reflect broader cultural trends in the United States as it finds itself embroiled deeper in political conflict with parts of the Islamic world.

When we examine the history of the veil in Hollywood, we see that the meaning of its imagery has evolved in often surprising ways as Americans have more contact, for good or ill, with Muslims. Personally, I see the veil as going through several stages that can be dated specifically in relation to world events. Prior to the 1970s, Muslim characters in films were not necessarily seen as villainous, and Islam itself was not perceived to be an enemy of Western civilization. But neither were Muslims seen as normal human beings who shared much in common with Western audiences. And the use of the veil as a prop in these films reflects this ambiguity.

During that pre-1970s era (often called the "Golden Age of Hollywood"), Muslim characters in film fell into two kinds of categories. First, they were larger-than-life heroes with mystical, otherworldly lives, as symbolized by the early efforts to adapt the medieval Arabian Nights tales into film. These movies ranged from the original *Thief of Baghdad* (1924) starring Douglas Fairbanks, to *Ali Baba and the Forty Thieves* (1944), to *The Seventh Voyage of Sinbad* (1958), which showcased cutting edge stop-motion animation from special effects pioneer Ray Harryhausen. In these films, Muslims were adventurous and honorable people who nonetheless lived in a magical reality far removed from the modern world of science and reason. And veiled women onscreen were symbolic of this otherworldliness that made them as strange and inaccessible to the Western audience as the *djinnis* that often came to rescue the heroes. The veil was in essence a prop, like the magical lamp of Aladdin, to showcase how different the Muslim world was from the modern West.

Thief of Baghdad

The second type of "Golden Age" portrayals of Islam were more rooted in earthly reality, but provided a chance for Westerners to project their own racial prejudices and secret desires on to the Muslim characters. Muslims in such films were not necessarily magical, but were seen as representing a forbidden allure and sexuality that simmered in the American subconscious prior to the Sexual Revolution of the 1960s. In films as far back as 1921's *The Sheik,* starring Rudolph Valentino, Muslims were seen as debauched and hyper-sexed, sensually lounging about harems overflowing with wine and beautiful concubines. The veiled women in such films were temptresses and belly dancers, using the lure of the hidden to seduce and titillate. And thus the veil in such films became an object of erotic fantasy for a society in which sexuality was heavily repressed.

This view of Muslims as the mysterious "other" was thus very much in place by the 1970s when global political events suddenly pushed Islam into the daily consciousness of Americans. The defining media events about Muslims during that time were the oil embargo of the 1970s that caused huge lines for Americans daily at the gas pump, and shocking news stories such as the rash of airplane hijackings by Palestinians desperate to bring attention to the injustices against their people.

Suddenly Muslims were the mysterious "other" again, but not as magical warriors or romantic sheiks. Rather they were now rich and heartless oil barons, or ruthless terrorists. And the portrayal of Muslims in film shifted accordingly. But even in these instances, the veil was used to signify the "otherness" of Muslims, with a newly negative connotation added to the simple strip of cloth. The veil became a symbol of the barbaric and cruel culture that Islam suddenly possessed in the media's eyes. Even fantasy shows like the 1970s *Bionic Woman* followed the new narrative, with an episode in which Jaime Sommers fights off villainous Arab goons to protect a playboy prince, who shows his gratitude to the heroine by promising to treat his veiled (i.e. – oppressed) wife as an equal from now on. Jaime Sommers' victory against the bad guys was symbolized by her victory against the veil.

This trend would continue and worsen for the next several decades as political events created an even worse perception of Muslims in the media. The Iranian Revolution and hostage crisis of the late 1970s soon relabelled Islam as not only decadent and cruel, but as fanatically irrational in its hostility to Western values. The veil became a symbol of the religious oppression of Muslim women in Iran, an image that reached its apogee in the 1991 film *Not Without My Daughter*, in which Sally Field played an American who tries to flee Iran with her child.

The ultimate nadir for American perceptions of Islam was, of course, the terrorist attacks of September 11, 2001. In the wake of the tragedy, many hate crimes were reported against Muslims, and Muslim women wearing the veil became easy targets for bigots. The veil had devolved first from a symbol of exotic and erotic "otherness", to a tool of oppression against Muslim women from which they needed to be liberated, and finally to the uniform worn by "the enemy", thus an existential threat to the American way of life. The images in Hollywood movies both followed the cultural trend, and shaped it. In recent days, TV shows like *Homeland* and *Tyrant* continue to strengthen the perception that Islam is a violent, misogynistic religion that is at odds with Western culture, and the veil is very much used as an automatic reference point for such ideas. In recent billboard advertisements for *Homeland*, for example, the heroine (played by Claire Danes) is shown wearing a brightly colored headscarf while walking in a mass of Muslim women clad in sinister black. The subliminal message for the spy show is clear – the American woman is different (and in danger) because she stands out from the veiled crowd.

And yet despite this negative trajectory, there is still hope that Hollywood can use the veil honestly to explore the complexities of Muslim culture and its relationship with the West. On *Sleeper Cell*, a Showtime Networks series I worked for as a writer and co-producer, we had a Muslim hero, an FBI agent who fought terrorists. My fellow producers on the show made an admirable effort to present a more normative version of Islam to challenge the negative stereotypes, including the presentation of Muslim women who were veiled and yet still served as positive characters. And other TV shows, ranging from *Seventh Heaven* to the short-lived family drama *Jack and Bobby*, had scenes in which American Muslim women defended wearing the veil in the face of mockery and bigotry by other characters.

Most recently, the ABC series *Quantico* features twin Muslim sisters training as FBI cadets. The sisters have different values. One is deeply religious, while the other is secular. The show has increasingly shown the differences in the two sisters' worldviews through their attitudes toward the veil. The religious sister dons it proudly, while the other disdains the headscarf. The storyline represents an effort to show a range of perspectives on the issue that approximates to the actual discussions that Muslim women are having today, and thus represents progress in Hollywood on the issue.

While all of the TV shows I mention above remain the exception toward the standard stereotypes, the very fact that they are now appearing in Hollywood suggests that perceptions are changing again as more Americans interact with Muslims and see their point of view in daily life.

The veil thus serves both to hide, and to highlight. It is a signifier that reveals how attitudes toward Muslims have evolved and continue to evolve as the world changes. With the beginning of a new age of global connection and information sharing, it is inevitable that cultural attitudes toward the veil will continue to shift, and that the media will eventually present a more balanced perspective on the issue. The greatest irony of the veil is that it unveils what is hidden inside people's hearts, which is the starting point of dialogue. It is a conversation in which Hollywood will continue to play a powerful role. But it is ultimately up to Muslims to participate in these venues and make sure their voices are included in how the media crafts their image to the world.

Which raises the final issue to consider. How can the image of Muslims in general and the veil in particular be improved within Hollywood? The only way there will be lasting and effective change is for Muslims to become actively involved in the film industry. After fifteen years, I remain one of only a few Muslims who are members of the Writers Guild of America, the professional union for Hollywood screenwriters. In my experience, Muslims remain reluctant to enter the media field, partly through lack of professional guidance and connections that would make such a career seem realistic, and partly due to insecurity and fear of failure. The American Muslim community still traps itself within negative thinking, believing that the only careers available to us are within "practical" professions such as medicine and engineering. This mindset has caused an entire generation of Muslims to forgo their dreams and live their lives according to a self-created sense of limitation.

Only when Muslims begin to take risks and expand beyond a narrowly defined paradigm for their own lives can there be any meaningful change within how the broader society perceives them. The fact that Muslims have been the primary targets for misrepresentation by Hollywood and the media, and yet remain wilfully outside the very system that defines public opinion, reflects a failure of courage and imagination within the community. In truth, we Muslims have abdicated our responsibility for shifting the media narrative, and until we lift the barrier that we have created in our own minds towards participating in Hollywood, we shall continue to suffer from a worsening public attitude that has resulted in the rise of anti-Muslim demagogues like the current presidential candidate Donald Trump.

Glossary of Terms

Abaya: long robes used as cover over other clothes.

Ahmaddiyah: a disenfranchised community which has been labelled non-Muslim by mainstream Muslim populations.

Alhamdulillah: Praise be to God.

Allah-u-akbar: God is great.

Almirah: Closet.

Assalamu'Alaykum: Peace be upon you.

Baaligh: a Muslim child that has reached the age of maturity.

Buloogh: transition from childhood to adulthood, when one takes on responsibility for religious obligations.

Burka: outerwear that covers a woman from head to toe, including usually the face.

Burkini: bathing suit that fully covers the body.

Chador: long shawl or sheet used as a modest cover.

Chai: tea with milk.

Corniche: coastal area or beach.

Dawah: educating people on Islam.

Djinn: mystical beings that are part of the creation of God, according to the Quran. Satan belongs to this class of beings.

Dorji: tailor.

Dua: prayer or supplication.

Duhr Salat: afternoon prayer.

Dupatta: long scarf worn with South Asian clothing.

Eid: Muslim holidays that commemorate either the end of Ramadan or the completion of the Hajj pilgrimage.

Ghūnghaṭa: Hindi word for veil that is used to cover a woman's head and/or face.

Hadiths: sayings of the Prophet Muhammad (PBUH), also known as Sunnah.

Haik: a large outer wrap typically worn by people in North Africa.

Hajj: Muslim pilgrimage to Mecca that occurs only at specified times of the year; one of the five pillars of Islam.

Halal: Arabic word for permitted or lawful.

Haram: Arabic word for forbidden.

Hijab: Islamic headscarf; the practice of modesty in Islam.

Iftar: the breaking of the fast at sunset during Ramadan.

InshaAllah: God willing.

Istikhara: a specific prayer for guidance when a Muslim is ambivalent or unsure about a decision.

Itar: a natural perfume derived from botanical sources.

Jannah: the Islamic concept of paradise or heaven; in Arabic, literally translated to mean garden.

Jellaba: long loose-fitting unisex robe with full sleeves, often worn in North Africa.

Khaleeji: Gulf Arab.

Khap: an organization or council made up of clans or groups of related clans in northern India that is separate from elected government but can exert significant social influence in its local community.

Khimr: headscarf worn in Arabia at the time of the Prophet.

Kippa: Hebrew word for skullcap.

Kurta: tunic.

Lāja: Hindi word for modesty.

Lengha: long Indian skirt.

MashaAllah: Arabic phrase to express joy, praise, or thankfulness for something or someone that was just mentioned.

MENA: Middle East and North Africa region.

Muhajjabah: Muslim women who wear the hijab.

Muslimah: a Muslim woman.

Naan: Round tandoori bread.

Nani: maternal grandmother.

Niqab: face veil.

Payot: Hebrew work for side locks or side curls, worn by men and boys in the Orthodox Jewish community.

Quran: Muslim holy book.

Rajshahi: a region in Bangladesh.

Ramadan: holy month in Islam that is spent fasting from dawn to sunset and reflecting on moral and religious obligations.

Revert (to Islam): used by many Muslims as a substitute for the term "convert" to refer to the Islamic belief that people are born with an innate belief in God and in accepting Islam, they revert to their original state of submission.

Roti: Indo-Pakistani flat bread.

Sabr: patience.

Sadaqa: act of charity.

Sahih Bukhari: one of the Hadiths.

Salaam: a common greeting in Arabic-speaking and Muslim countries.

Salat: Muslim ritual prayers.

Sarma: Hindi word literally meaning shame but can be used to mean shyness.

Shahada: declaration of faith in Islam in which supplicants recite "There is no god but Allah and Muhammad is the messenger of Allah".

Shalwar Kameez: traditional Indian and Pakistani attire consisting of a long tunic over loose trousers and a scarf.

Shayla: headscarf, usually black, worn with the abaya.

Sitar: a stringed instrument belonging the the lute family which is popular in Indian music.

Sola Scriptura: a Christian doctrine that the Bible is the supreme authority in all matters of belief and practice.

Souq: Arab outdoor market.

SubhanAllah: Arabic phrase, literally meaning Glory to God, used as an exclamation.

Sunnah: the body of traditional, social and legal customs based on the teachings and practices of the prophet Muhammad.

Surah: chapter in the Quran.

Tabla: a percussion instrument consisting of two hand drums which is popular in Indian music.

Tahajjud: voluntary nightly prayers that are in addition to the 5 required Muslim prayers.

Ummah: Muslim community.

Umrah: pilgrimage to Mecca that is considered the lesser pilgrimage to Hajj.

Wahabism: a puritanical movement in Islam.

Zakat: obligatory charity, one of the five pillars of Islam.

Notes on the Editors and Contributors

The Editors

Nausheen Pasha-Zaidi has degrees in Communications, Education and Psychology. She has worked as an international educator for almost 20 years, focusing on language development and cultural studies, with an emphasis on Muslim populations. Her articles have appeared in a number of professional journals, including *Ethnicities* and *The Journal of International Women's Studies*. She is the author of *The Colour of Mehndi*, a novel exploring acculturation, family values and mental illness within the Pakistani-American community.

Shaheen Pasha is an assistant professor of international journalism at the University of Massachusetts, Amherst. She has been a journalist for over 15 years. Her work has appeared in publications such as *The Wall Street Journal*, Thomson Reuters, CNNMoney, *Quartz*, *The Daily Beast* and *USA Today*.

The Contributors

Ansha Zaman is a young Bengali professional with plans of pursuing a master's degree in the field of environmental sciences and natural resources.

Zahra Cheema is the founder of the law firm "Cheema and Associates", in New York. She has been heavily involved in the Muslim community for over seven years and continues actively to participate in local mosques and charity organizations.

Muneera Williams is a Bristol-born, London-based rapper and poet. She is one half of the hip-hop and spoken word duo, Poetic Pilgrimage. The group has performed around England and Europe, and has toured South Africa, Morocco and the United States. She is currently studying for her MA in Islamic studies, in which she is focusing on the Caribbean contribution to Islam, migration, gender and race.

Farhana N. Shah is an educator in the US. She earned her master's in Education, with a focus in Administration, from Loyola College in Maryland.

She uses her personal time to provide consultation, trainings and workshops to local private schools.

Nadia Eldemerdash is a writer living in Las Vegas. Nadia works in communications and writes about immigration and minority issues in the United States and the Middle East.

Skifou F. was born and raised in the diverse culture of Morocco. She has a degree in translation and has been teaching English as a second language for the last ten years. Her interests revolve around teaching and learning languages.

Cassie (Nadiya) Madison is a revert to Islam, a proud hijabi, a member of the Muslimah Writers Alliance, and an interfaith activist.

Maryam Nasser is a Tanzanian citizen who is currently pursuing her Post-Graduate Diploma in Business Management, under the UK based ABE qualification.

Saadia Faruqi is an interfaith activist, writer and speaker specializing in Muslim American issues. She is the author of *Brick Walls: Tales of Hope and Courage from Pakistan* (FB Publishing, 2015).

Faizah Malik is a freelance writer and the owner of the online accessories boutique Kenze (www.facebook.com/KenzeJewellery). She enjoyed a ten-year career in publishing before embarking on other ventures, including charity work and her own fashion business. She lives in Milton Keynes, England and is currently the Fashion Writer for www.MuslimMums.co.uk. Her blog, The Treasure Box, can be found at http://thetreasurebox-lavender.blogspot.co.uk.

Aida Othman is a qualified Chartered Accountant by profession with experience in banking and financial services. She calls several cities home, including Auckland, Sydney, Dubai and Singapore. She is the creator of the lifestyle, fitness and health blog, SliceOfTorchGinger.com, where she merges her interest in writing and social media. As an endurance runner, she aims to take on destination runs to combine her passion for travel and competing.

Zehra Naqvi is an attorney, community organizer, and writer. She has collaborated with a number of organizations on interfaith, intrafaith, and minority-focused initiatives, and frequently speaks on issues relating to faith, community outreach, and Islamophobia.. Zehra has written for a number of online publications, including the *Huffington Post*, *Refinery29*, and *Muharram in Manhattan*.

E. Dawson Varughese is a global cultural studies scholar and creative practitioner. She employs ethnographic methods in her research and is particularly interested in the encoding of post-millennial cultures in visual and literary productions. Her research specialism is India. See her work: www.beyondthepostcolonial.com.

Louise Lambert is a registered psychologist in Canada, and founder of the *Middle East Journal of Positive Psychology*. She developed the Happiness 101 series, a program designed for greater happiness in people who are flourishing, languishing, or depressed. She has lived in the UAE since 2010 and is interested in the study of happiness and culture, as well as the development of an indigenous positive psychology across the Middle East.

Caitlin Elaine is pursuing a masters in Middle Eastern Archaeology while living in the Middle East.

Patreshia Tkach has worked and lived in several countries including France, Turkey, the United Arab Emirates, and the United States. She teaches English language, writing, intercultural communication, and photography.

Dragana Randelovic is an architect engineer originally from Serbia. She currently lives in Abu Dhabi with her family and works as a lecturer at the Petroleum Institute.

Nell Green currently serves as Field Personnel with the Cooperative Baptist Fellowship. She has experience working with Muslims in Africa and Europe. For the past few years she has been helping churches in North America develop multidisciplinary ministries to meet the needs of international communities.

Dr. Fawzia Mai Tung is a Chinese Muslim from Taiwan, and has been wearing the hijab for over thirty years. A retired psychiatrist, journalist and educator, she currently lives in the USA.

T. Akhtar was born and raised in Karachi, Pakistan. She completed her MBA and worked in the corporate sector for a few years. She is currently living in Saudi Arabia.

Scotty Enyart is a licensed psychotherapist from California and holds a Ph.D. in psychology with a focus on comparative psychologies. His research interest in indigenous healing practices has taken him to Eastern Africa, Japan, Australia, New Zealand, and Central and South America. Dr Enyart currently works for the US Federal government in Asia providing counseling to bicultural families.

Yvonne El Ashmawi is an assistant professor of middle and secondary

English Education at Loyola University, Chicago. A few of her research interests are multicultural young adult fiction, teaching writing for social justice, Chicana Muslims in public schools, and Chicana Feminism.

Kathryn Kraft is lecturer in International Development at the University of East London. She has worked in various countries across the Middle East and the wider Arab world, as well as Southeast Asia, Haiti and West Africa, engaged in a variety of initiatives to empower local civil society and support peacebuilding and interfaith dialogue.

Sukhdev Singh teaches English at the National Institute of Technology in Patna, Bihar (India). His scholarly research is primarily concerned with sex and gender studies. He is an award-winning writer of short stories, poems, and one-act plays.

Carrie York Al-Karam is an adjunct professor at the University of Iowa. She conducts research, publishes, and teaches on psychology and religion, Islamic psychology, and spiritually integrated psychotherapy. She spent nearly 17 years outside of her native US in various countries, including 10 years in the United Arab Emirates.

Laila Dahan was born and raised in Tripoli, Libya. She holds MAs in political science and TESOL and a Ph.D. in language education. She taught writing at the American University of Sharjah in the UAE for over thirteen years, and is currently an independent scholar and editor who publishes in a wide-range of interdisciplinary fields.

Angelika Böck is a visual artist and interior architect. Her work deals with phenomena of human perception, and contains elements from both art and research derived from field studies within different cultural settings. She currently lives and works in Munich (Germany) and Bario (Sarawak/Malaysia) and is a Ph.D. candidate at the Centre for Transcultural Research and Media Practice at Dublin Institute of Technology (Ireland).

Carol Tandava Henning has worked on stage as an actor, director, writer, producer, bellydancer, theatrical improviser, and stand-up comic. She is best known for her solo show, *Blood on the Veil*, which has toured throughout the U.S. Her work is strongly influenced by Joseph Campbell, Jungian psychology, and archetypal principals.

N.B. Sky is a beauty and wellness professional who has worked in most areas of the beauty industry over the past fifteen years. Her mission is to teach women around the world that they can look and feel good using natural products and foods that promote health and wellness.

Kamran Pasha is a Hollywood filmmaker and author of two novels on Islamic history, *Mother of the Believers* and *Shadow of the Swords*.

Mirror on the veil : a collection of
personal essays on hijab and veiling

BP 190.5 .H44 M57 2017 cop.1

2018

DATE DUE

St mary's Uofpw

ILL 2019 2/14 Fitzgerald	

PRINTED IN U.S.A.

Made in the USA
Lexington, KY
16 August 2018